Praise for the best-selling *Motley Fool UK Investment Guide*

"(The book) is geared entirely to the UK market and it is difficult to see how anyone could fail to benefit." *Mail on Sunday*

". . . a thoroughly entertaining read . . . It shows the novice investor and the expert alike how to take full control of their investing future and how to have fun doing it." *The Investor*

"This book may not save you a fortune, but it could just make you one." *amazon.co.uk*

"As a guide for the novice the book is an excellent starting point" *Computer Shopper*

"I can thoroug *l UK*
Investment Guia fully
invest your mon ner,
spiced with a bit

. . . and for the *Motley Fool UK* web site, winner of the 1999 *New Media Age* Award for Best Personal Finance web site and the 1999 *Creative Freedom* Best Electronic Media Site

". . . provides a good grounding in the share-dealing basics for investors who are new to the stock market game." *The Daily Telegraph*

"The brilliant Motley Fool achieves just the right balance between humour and hard-nosed research to make playing the market fun as well as, hopefully, profitable." *The Sun*

"The financial future is bright and easier to understand, thanks to The Motley Fool." *Business Age*

"What the Motley Fool says can have an impact on the biggest stock markets in the world." *The Scotsman*

"Cool. Actually quite hip." *Wired Magazine*

"It stands out as an ethical oasis in the area that is fast becoming home to charlatans." *The Economist*

"The Motley Fool site offers excellent information in an irreverent and friendly style." *Computeractive*

The following Motley Fool books are also published by Boxtree:

The Motley Fool UK Investment Guide
The Motley Fool UK Investment Workbook
The Fool's Guide to Online Investing (available soon)

The Fool's Guide To Investment Clubs

Mark Goodson with David Berger

First published 1999 by Boxtree
an imprint of Macmillan Publishers Ltd
25 Eccleston Place, London, SW1W 9NF
Basingstoke and Oxford

www.macmillan.co.uk

Associated companies throughout the world

ISBN 0 7522 1811 5

9 8 7 6 5 4 3 2 1

A CIP catalogue record for this book is available from the British Library.

Typeset by SX Composing DTP, Rayleigh, Essex
Printed in Great Britain by Mackays of Chatham plc, Kent

Contents

Foreword

The thing about FatBlokeMarge was that he wasn't fat. Granted, he wasn't tremendously thin, either, but he certainly wasn't fat. We were meeting him for the first time at a meeting room we'd hired for a Motley Fool pow-wow in London in early 1999 (this was because we had no offices at the time – the Fool was still an entirely virtual organization).

Mark – for FatBlokeMarge* was just the screen name by which we knew him from his regular postings on the Fool online message boards – had been invited along to have a chat about writing *The Fool's Guide to Investment Clubs.* Meeting people in the flesh who one knows solely from the online environment is always an adventure, but apart from the incongruity of the 'FatBloke' tag, there was no surprise about Mark. We already knew from his postings that he ran several investment clubs, that he was a down-to-earth sort of person, a Fool and a regular good fellow. It was also

*There is a story behind this name, but it was long, convoluted and, I think, involved a ski trip, a dead donkey and the bishop's daughter. Or something like that. You'll have to ask Mark about it directly.

clear that he was uncommonly good at motivating people. With three clubs currently on the go, he was being besieged to start another and at the time of writing has another two clubs due to start in several months that are already fully subscribed. With another waiting list already filling up, this rate of growth means that the entire population of Essex is going to be a member of one of Mark's investment clubs by around April 2002. Ah well, there are worse fates indeed.

We were delighted when he agreed to write this book, as we thought his style, his positive approach to life, already evident in his postings, and his extraordinary powers of inspiration were going to lend a vibrancy to a subject which doesn't excite as many people as it justly should. That may be because they haven't yet heard of investment clubs, or if they have that they know the name only and associate them with stuffiness.

Nothing could be further from the truth.

Investment clubs are an excellent way of getting out of the house, meeting with friends, pulling the sides of your mouth up into that vital everyday activity known as a 'smile' and learning about shares and investing. We encourage them very strongly at the Fool and hopefully this book will encourage you to consider starting or joining one. It's not a manual, however. ProShare, a non-profit organization which you will hear about throughout this book, does a very good job in producing an extensive manual which every investment club should buy. Instead, this book is more a collection of Mark's stories and insights from five years of running investment clubs, laced with a whiff of Foolishness, all designed to give you the *feel* of what it may be like to be part of a club and take part in regular meetings. It's also full of many hard-won tips on how to keep a club thriving, how to help everyone take part and – this is **important** – stay friends. Mark describes himself as 'the most reasonable man on earth', which I can confirm is the case and which comes through as one of the key factors in the success or otherwise of an investment club. There has to be a lot of give-and-take, tolerance and reasonableness in all members for a club to work. (Hang on, doesn't that go for just about any cooperative human activity?)

It's dangerous to give guarantees in life, but I can give you one here: you will enjoy this book, which is infinitely more of a story than a treatise, and it will make you think seriously about starting an investment club. Even if you don't go on to start one, though, you'll have gained some useful insights, had a chuckle and understood what it is that motivates otherwise normal, sane individuals to venture out on a cold November evening just before the *Nine o'Clock News* to an investment club meeting.

A potted history of the Motley Fool, you ask? Why certainly, good Fool! There have already been quite a lot of 'Fools' and 'Foolishness' floating around so far, so we'd better explain what and who we are. The Motley Fool was founded in the US in 1993 by brothers David and Tom Gardner. This was in response to the gross overcharging and shocking underperformance of the mainstream financial services industry, of so-called "Wise" investment managers. If this was Wisdom, reckoned David and Tom, why we're just Fools, but surely Fools can do better than this? Why should Fools not be able to manage their own money and, with their contrary, refreshing position, do better than the Wise? Is there some kind of masonic initiation and secret knowledge you have to have to be able to look after your own investments? No. And the sad truth – true in the UK too – is that over 90 per cent of American professional money managers failed to beat the average performance of the stock market over five-year periods.

With a background like this, the time was long overdue for a revolution in the style of the Shakespearean Fool: belled cap a-jingling, pointing out the absurd when no-one else dare and educating as he amuses. 'Ye Olde Printed Foole', as it is fondly now known, started off as a print newsletter circulated to family and friends, way back in the mists of . . . 1993. Mythology tells us it had a circulation of 60 in that first month, mostly family and friends. This shot up, however, when portions of its humorous and educational content were posted on new-fangled online message boards, where it attracted comment and readers from all over the US. From there it was just a short hop, step and a jump to a regular slot on AOL, the online service, where it became increasingly popular. Fuelled by the dedicated community of investors – Fools – who thronged its message boards, the Foolish phenomenon has snowballed. Now, the online areas of the US Motley Fool – both on AOL and on the Web at www.fool.com – have several million visitors a month, there is a series of best-selling US Fool books, with over a million in print, a national radio show, a newspaper column in over 130 US newspapers and – pause for breath – now a Foolish presence in Europe.

In early 1997 I was an avid reader and occasional contributor to the US Fool site. It's fair to say I was hooked. Utterly. So hooked, so keen that I emailed David and Tom one grey, rainy Devon afternoon, mooting a UK Fool. In a trice – OK, in three months – I was America-bound and hatching plans for a British version. Shortly after that, in September 1997, the UK site was launched, also on AOL and later on the World Wide Web, with myself and another UK Fool, Bruce Jackson, at the helm. (At the helm? We were *it*!) We were running it in the evenings, as we were both still doing our respective day jobs, putting out eight articles a week between us (insane, yes, but strangely it felt OK at the time). Since then, the Foolish phenomenon has taken root in Britain, aided by the rapid growth in Internet use over the last year or so and a general realization that if you don't look after your own money, no-one else is going to do it for you. The traffic at the Motley Fool's UK website, www.fool.co.uk, is doubling approximately every three months and *The Motley Fool UK Investment Guide*, published in October 1998, continues to sell heartwarmingly well. British Fools are realizing that they can invest for themselves, that you don't have to be a brain surgeon to understand the basics of investing and that long-term wealth beckons to the steady, patient investor.

As I write this, the half-finished, dog-eared manuscript for *The Motley Fool UK Investment Workbook*, co-authored by Bruce Jackson and myself, is also due for delivery in just two weeks. Oh dearie, dearie me! (Adrian – he's our publisher at Boxtree – if you're reading this, I'm really sorry both these books were late. We'll try not to disappoint you again. Honest.) What that means is that I'm going to crib some principles of Foolishness which I jotted down on the fly for that book for the foreword to this one. So what follows are just a few thoughts on what Foolishness may be all about to the many people who take part in this collaborative enterprise . . .

Enjoying Life

Well, you have to, don't you?

Nurturing a Foolish Approach to Investing
It makes so much more sense in the long run, because the long run is what it's all about. By being Foolish and developing a Foolish attitude, one of investing on the basis of common sense, evidence and sound fundamentals, you really will be able to provide for your future with so much less stress.

Sorting Out Your Own Goals and Risk Tolerances
No-one knows these like you. Certainly, no paid adviser can know these. Once you have them sorted out, it will give you far more directional focus when you know in which direction to channel your energies, investing and otherwise.

The Best Things in Life are Free
Including the Fool, the companionship of others and the thrill of being alive.

Getting Out of Debt
Credit card debt, especially, is a killer of investment returns. Get rid of it before you start investing.

The Power of Time and the Miracle of Compounding
Give your savings time to grow and the effect will astonish you.

The Power of the Stock Market
The companies making up the stock market, the

driving force behind our economy, are by far the most effective place to grow your savings over the long term.

The Power of the Individual
You can do it. You really can.

The Power of Community
Especially if you have other people to help you.

The heart of both the UK and US websites is the message board area. Here, Fools from all over the world exchange ideas and views, with the twin aims of enjoying themselves and learning about money and investing at the same time. In many ways, those boards serve a social function, with communities of investors getting together on different boards and getting to know each other well as they conduct conversations over days, weeks or months. While the extraordinary diversity of informed opinion available from millions of people online can never be matched by a group of ten to twenty people in an investment club, similarly the online environment can never tell you whether the bloke who calls himself 'FatBloke' really is or the girl who calls herself 'CuddlyFool' isn't telling a big fib. And sometimes, that kind of thing is important.

So, in signing off, what can I say, but . . .

Be a Fool, start an investment club.

Take it away, FatBlokeMarge!

David Berger
Baker Street, London, June 1999

Introduction

'And the winner of the 1998 ProShare Achievement Award is . . . H+G Investments!'

Oh, my head! 25 February 1999, and what a hangover! The day before had been a proud day. We had done it. We merry few, the H+G Investment Club, had won the 1998 ProShare Achievement Award. That meant a trophy and a cheque for £1500. The trophy, of course, meant lots of polishing, but the cheque meant a liquid celebration was in order. Now, where were those aspirins again?

How little of this we had foreseen in those darkening November days of 1994, when H+G first took shape. No-one, especially yours truly, could have known how popular and successful it was going to be.

The stock market had long held a fascination for me, but I did not have much of a handle on how it worked. I, like many others, had made a few bob on the government privatization issues, like British Gas and British Telecom, but other than that my only other ventures into the market had met with disaster. My first real investment was in Millwall Football Club in 1993. I'm not a fan, but with a new stadium, promises of income from other sources, such as pop concerts and the like, and a team in the Division 1 play-offs, the shares seemed a good bet at just 3.75p. If they got into the Premiership, the shares would leap to about 10p, surely? They were in good form, too. Wrong! They lost in the play-offs to Derby County and were later relegated to Division 2, where they currently languish. The shares now stand at 1p each.

My second investment was in mid-1994 and was based on a 'hot tip' from a client. Sycamore Holdings was the company, and the shares were 0.75p to buy. Stock market prices are generally measured in quarters of a penny, so a single movement upwards meant a 33 per cent increase in the price. And they couldn't go any lower, surely . . . ?

One lunchtime I checked the price on Ceefax and was staggered to see it standing at 23p. Yes, 23p. A massive increase!! Out came the calculator. I really fancied a new car; we could go on holiday . . . hold on, what about Capital Gains Tax? Quick, check the situation with my broker. I could barely contain my excitement, but you know how you sometimes get that feeling that something really is too good to be true? Like winning a big prize and not actually believing it until you are holding it in your hands?

On this occasion I was right to have doubts. My broker quickly brought me down to earth by telling me that Sycamore had reorganized their capital in a

1-for-100 issue that morning. This meant that shareholders now held only one share for every 100 they held before. My very modest investment of £500 had turned into about £165. The shares are currently 2.5p and the amount I'd get for selling them wouldn't even cover the dealing costs. Remember this story the next time someone tells you that a company's share price cannot possibly get any cheaper. As we'll see later, too, these kinds of penny shares make for poor long-term investments.

With a wife, two children, a very small private pension and no capital, I began looking in the early 1990s at ways of trying to provide for my long-term future. Since the Maxwell saga I had lost faith in pensions completely. I wanted to control my own money and my own future. It was in the late summer of 1994 that an experience made very plain to me how far customers of financial institutions were being, well, short-changed, to say the least. I was at a dinner party with friends and they had invited their neighbours, one of whom managed funds in the equities market for a major household name in the banking sector. He was what we at the Motley Fool call 'One of the Wise'. I was interested in what he was saying, and asked if he had had any really bad days, Nick Leeson* days. 'Sure,

*The trader who brought down Barings Bank through his unauthorised trading activities and massive losses.

we all do,' he replied, 'although not quite that bad.' I asked what happened when large losses occurred, and was told that they were essentially passed on to the customer. In my naivety, I countered by saying that obviously this was compensated for by the very good days. 'Not exactly,' I was told, 'because the bank can only employ me if I make a profit for them, so a lot of the profits are kept by the bank. If they passed all the profits back, I'd be out of a job.' From a business point of view, perhaps this is understandable. The bank does have to make a profit, and of course they have to employ these 'Wise' people to manage the funds for the customers who give them their money to make an investment return and hopefully a profit. But hang on a minute! *All* the losses are passed back, while only *some* of the profits are retained? That means that if the bank loses, the customer loses, but if the bank wins, then the customer only wins if the bank wins enough first. Hmm . . .

Shortly after this conversation I read an article about investment clubs in one of the national Sunday papers. Now, this looked like a good idea! The average outlay seemed to be about £25 per month (doesn't burn too much of a hole in the pocket, does it?) and the clubs tended to consist of groups of friends who held their meetings in a pub. What's more, these clubs were making 20 to 25 per cent per year profit! And with no fund managers to pay. OK, often they were also putting money across the bar in the pub in the course of their meetings, but they were actually getting a good return on their money and having a bit of a social life at the same time. This really did seem too good to be true.

I wrote down the names of fourteen friends who I thought might be interested in forming a club, contacted them, and twelve took me up on the offer. We met in the 'Horse and Groom' in Rochford, Essex. 'H+G' it was, then. Lucky we weren't regulars at the Sloth and Marmoset.

Investment clubs are no joke, they're not just for a bit of small-time amateur dabbling. No, they are serious financial vehicles. When I eventually retire (I'll be 65 in 2026), what's left of the state pension isn't going to buy much in the way of tea bags and cat food, not to mention supporting the bar at the Horse and Groom. Investment clubs provide a cheap, efficient way of saving, an opportunity to get out with friends once a month, and they give individuals the knowledge and, more importantly, the confidence to invest in the stock market for themselves. For those who have already come close to drowning in bad investments before, a club can be a way back into the water, but with water-wings this time.

I am better at investing these days, and I am in much firmer control of my financial destiny. There is no big secret to investment, no matter what the 'Wise' may say. There is, for them, a strong incentive to make it hard for us. They use strange words and talk in magical incantations so that we will put our faith in them and they in turn can cream off a tidy profit for themselves. This book, then, aims to help defrock such pretenders, and make it easy for individuals to do it for themselves, through the agency of that wonderful invention, the investment club.

And who knows, it might crack your fizzog into a smile or two along the way.

1

What's with the book?

Let us be thankful for the Fools. But for them the rest of us could not succeed.
Mark Twain

OK, hands up all those people who never read the introductions to books, then. Yes, the game's up. You're nobbled. You missed the overview of Foolishness, didn't you? And you don't know what inspired the author to start out on the long and Foolish road that ended with a host of investment clubs either, do you? Well, stop right there! Fools never start out without making maximum use of the information available to them. So, go back a few pages and start reading again, Fool.

Back with us now? Enjoy that? OK, let's continue.

What kind of person can actually get down to it and successfully run a profitable investment club? It must take some sort of relevant education, a career in the City, nobby friends with 'insider' tips, and a stripy shirt and wide braces, mustn't it? No, no, no, Fools! It just takes an ordinary person, a clear vision and a bit of common sense.

Look at our own example, a bloke with a Foolish screen name that makes him sound like a rotund transvestite. Born in 1961 (not old, just maturing nicely), with a wife and three kids, five 'O' levels, and a career spanning retail banking (no, not a Wise position, just a bank branch junior), the travel industry, the dole, and who ended up as a Registered Trust and Estate Practitioner (that's wills, trusts, and probate to ordinary folk, nothing too Wise there either). Is this the kind of unlikely-sounding individual who you would expect to be able to start an investment club in November 1994 and see it grow to accumulate assets in excess of £30,000 less than four years later? Well, that's what happened, and that thirty grand represented a near doubling of the club's money, invested by individual subscriptions of a mere £25 per member, per month. Less than four years. Not bad, eh? Anyone who can afford the fiver or so it cost to buy this book can surely afford to save £25 per month. After all, our futures depend on our own savings. We need the money to buy that rocking chair, and all those slippers and cardigans (or maybe that yacht, and all those holidays, for those who do better than average).

The H+G club was started with nothing. (Don't know what the H+G club is? You didn't read that introduction after all, did you?) Really, absolutely nothing, not a sausage, b- (*That's enough Monty Python quotes for now. Ed.*). You don't need a lump sum to start a club. All it took was an initial joining fee of £25 per member (there are some modest start-up costs to take into account, after all) and then monthly subscriptions, paid in advance. It took three months to accumulate enough money to buy anything at all. That was good, though, because it gave the members enough time to think about it carefully, to do a bit of homework, and learn something about stock market investing. You see, at the start, the combined knowledge of the club amounted to nothing, not a sau- (*I've told you once. Ed.*).

So this was a club of complete beginners. Total novices. But those are exactly the sort of people who can successfully run investment clubs.

Let's digress from starting up an investment club for a moment. Here's a quick taster of what you might expect, just to whet your appetite. Suppose you, and a bunch of friends, put £25 per month into a club, and you do this for 25 years, never cashing it in, never taking any money out. How would you have done? It depends on the returns you get, of course, but suppose you average 20 per cent per year (that is, admittedly, quite a lot, but backtesting of the Motley Fool's Beating the Dow strategy in the US, and Beating the Footsie strategy in the UK show that this kind of return is achievable, over the long run). How much will you have then? What will your personal share be worth? You'll have around £250,000. A quarter of a million pounds! And what if you achieve 25 per cent per year (OK, that may be stretching it a bit, but let's just see)? That would get you a massive £850,000, give or take a few thousand quid. You may not manage 25 per cent, of course, but it does show what a difference those extra few per cent every year can make. Next time you have a financial salesperson telling you that a couple of per cent in charges on your investment every year is reasonable, you'll know differently, won't you?

Where the US leads, the UK tends to follow

In the United States of America, there is only minimal state support for non-earners. In fact, people don't really fare well at all on what Americans refer to as 'welfare'.

Americans need to be a lot more financially self-sufficient than the Brits, then. So are we safe and comfy here, with the state to support us when we need it? Oh, no. The truth is that today's working people will be in a pretty similar boat to our American friends before long. Standards of living are forever increasing, with more and more of yesterday's luxuries becoming today's necessities, and it all costs money. Medical advances made over the last ten to fifteen years, and generally improving health mean that people are living longer. In the 1980s we entered the leisure age and we were encouraged to plan our retirement for 50 or 55. Wow, fantastic! All that time on the golf course, the holidays, think of the fun pensioners could have . . . but who is going to pay for it all? It won't be the state, that's for sure. Here's a story from a local pub from a few years ago that illustrates this quite dramatically. There was a gentleman at the bar, surrounded by friends and colleagues, and he was obviously delirious with delight. Either that or drunk. Thinking about it, definitely drunk.

Anyway, there he was, and it wasn't particularly busy in this place, so he generously offered to buy a round of drinks for everyone in the bar. A smart, elderly man was standing alongside at the bar and graciously accepted the offer. He asked what was being celebrated. 'I've just retired,' he was told, 'and I feel GREAT!' The happy man then spent the next few minutes relating how he was going to relax, travel the world, etc. etc. The old man listened, and then asked how old he was. 'Fifty-five,' he replied. 'I hope you've got a lot of money,' the old man retorted, 'because I'm eighty-five, and if you live to be my age, I can tell you it's a blooming long time without a bonus or a pay-rise.' Well, you've never seen someone's jaw hit the floor as fast before. This kindly, well-dressed pensioner's comments had hit one almighty nerve with this chap, who suddenly realized that perhaps he wouldn't be able to do all the wonderful things he had planned. Sobered him up pretty quick, it did.

Take control of your finances then, Fools. And the sooner the better.

Off-the-shelf financial products

Where should we put our money for our old age? The shelves of the Wise are full to overflowing with financial products that they'd love to sell us, but are they good enough for Fools? *The Motley Fool UK Investment Guide* covers such fiendish devices in much more detail than we have space for here, but here's a quick summary.

Pensions

We have seen all the adverts and the press coverage about the massive pension misselling scandals of the 1980s and 90s. Maybe you were even stung yourself. Hardly fills you with confidence, does it? There are tax benefits to pensions, but the high charges and poor performance of many private pensions often make them barely worthwhile, if at all. Pensions are heavily sold by 'Independent Financial Advisers' – mostly just salespeople really, and mostly not all that independent – who stand to make a killing in commission. And when you retire, what happens to your money? Why, the law insists that you buy an annuity with it. Read on . . .

Annuities

To buy an annuity, you simply hand over all of your cash (your pension savings, for example) to a Wise company. In return, they provide you with a lowly sum every month for the rest of your life. This sum, the annuity return, is invariably pretty poor as a percentage of your capital, often barely above a long-term building society rate. But the real sting is what happens to your cash. The company keeps it, that's what. And it doesn't matter how long you live either. If you die shortly after starting to draw your income, then that's it. *Phwwwt!* Gone. Your relatives get nothing. If pensioners were allowed to keep their money and invest it themselves, and if they did it Foolishly, they could expect a much more comfortable old age than an annuity will provide. And a nice legacy for the grandchildren, too.

Endowments

There has been a lot of press lately about endowment policy proceeds not being sufficient to repay the loans they are intended to cover, usually as part of a mortgage. Many endowment policies take over seven years before the value of the contributions paid in even equals the amount in the fund, so high are their charges. The chances are that you won't really know how well it has done until it matures, right at the end of its life. Endowments are also big favourites with 'Independent Financial Advisers'. Another killing in commission. *Ker-ching!*

Individual Savings Accounts (ISAs)

The government's attempt to get ordinary people to save and invest for their futures. Up to an annual limit, money can be invested in one of these (in cash, shares or insurance) and the returns are completely tax-free. The tax benefits mean that ISAs do have a valid place in long-term financial planning, although individual Capital Gains Tax allowance, and the ISA fees themselves, need to be balanced against the tax saved. Many off-the-shelf products that fall into this category – based on 'actively managed unit trusts', which employ highly paid managers to pick your stocks for you – often carry very high fees, and offer dismal underperformance. It is a sad fact that over 90 per cent of actively managed unit trusts do worse than the average performance of the stock market.

If you employ someone to manage your investments for you, then they have to be paid for the work they do. Fair enough. But the fees you pay are never linked to the performance of the managers. You pay if they win, you pay if they lose. If you are in an investment club and you sometimes lose money, you don't have to pay anyone for the privilege. And you keep all of the profits when you are doing well.

The finance industry speaks a different language

'WiseSpeak', that's the language. What is it all about, and why do they use it? Partly it is to make them seem important and to discourage ordinary people from thinking they can do it for themselves. Because they don't want that, no sir. That would eat into all those fat profits they make from commissions and fees every year. Every year that they underperform the market, that is. We do need to understand some of this babble, unfortunately. How else can we see through their sheep-like disguises and reveal them for the wolves they really are?

That is what the Motley Fool is all about, of course. In Elizabethan drama, the Fool was the one person who could tell the King the truth and still keep his head. The Motley Fool aims to make investment understandable, fun and within the grasp of ordinary people.

Another essential source of information is an extremely Foolish organization known as ProShare. A non-profit-making organization, ProShare is dedicated to helping people set up investment clubs. They won't help to choose your investments or manage your money, but they *will* provide you with all the information you need to get going. For a modest fee, a club can join ProShare, and get a copy of their *Investment Club Manual*, an essential reference for all new clubs, containing sample club rules, a specimen club constitution, and much more. Its pages are designed to be photocopied and distributed throughout the club. Everything you need to know is in there. Proshare can be found at

ProShare (UK) Limited
Library Chambers
13-14 Basinghall Street
London EC2V 5BQ
Telephone: 020 7600 0984
www.proshare.org.uk

2

Why invest in the stock market at all?

The only reason to invest in the market is because you think you know something others don't.
R. Foster Winans, a *Wall Street Journal* reporter, later convicted for insider trading

Even if we haven't all fallen for it, many of us have been offered the chance to fling ourselves headlong into the stock market on nothing more than a 'hot tip' from this really nice guy down the pub. You know, the one who's got the friend who belongs to a golf club and whose brother's fiancée had dinner with the secretary to the MD at Consolidated Amalgamations, and who reckons that a takeover bid is in the offing . . .

Usually, this kind of thing is just a rumour designed to artificially push up the share price for a short period. Unsuspecting punters who get taken in often find themselves losing a lot of money when the price comes crashing down.

Unlike Mr Winans, above, very few of us actually *do* know any secrets, and of those who do, 99 per cent are just too honest or too committed to their careers to risk being caught 'insider trading'. There are very strict laws against that sort of thing.

So, why do we invest in the stock market?

The answer is simple: if someone had invested £100 in a deposit account in 1918, it would have been worth £6521 in December 1997. Not a bad increase, or is it? If that canny investor had instead put that £100 into gilts (bonds issued by the British government) over the same period, then the investment would have become £10,652. Nearly 40 per cent more. That's better. But if, over the same period, £100 had been invested in the stock market, then what would the final figure be worth? Go on, have a guess. £20,000? £50,000? £100,000? What about £200,000? Let's get even more ridiculous and say £500,000. Wrong on all five counts. Using the figures from the *Barclays Capital Equity-Gilt Study* (a study of investment performance over this century), that £100, invested in the stock market in 1918, would have turned into more than **£1,000,000** today.

Don't forget, that period covered the great crash of 1929, the Second World War, and the ravages of the bear market of the early 1970s when the market dropped dramatically.

But isn't stock market investment risky?

What about all those brokers jumping out of tall buildings in 1929, then? How about all that money that Uncle Harry lost in the 1970s? Well, those were short-term phenomena. Investing in the stock market is risky in the short term, but short-term investing is for mugs, not Fools. Who really invests their entire life savings in shares on one day, at the top of the market? Nobody, that's who. At least, nobody with any sense. Over the decades of a human lifespan, regular investing of more modest amounts is the way to go. Certainly, sometimes that money will go in at a peak, but at other times it will go in at a trough too. And remember, you get more shares for the same money when the market is down, so your average buying price is actually helped by a few ups and downs.

Whenever you look at charts of the stock market over any historical period, there is one thing that you will always notice – the line starts in the bottom left-hand corner and ends in the top right-hand corner. And if you have a look at the last 30 years, how does the great 1970s bear market figure? It's a little wiggle near the bottom left, one that looks barely significant now.

You have reached a critical point in your investing learning now, so sit back for a moment, and take a deep breath. You are about to have the BIG SECRET revealed to you. Are you ready? OK, here it comes . . . Time. That's it, that's the lot, just 'time'. There's nothing difficult in that, and you don't need a highly paid adviser to tell you it. Fools only invest money that they are not going to need for at least five years.

Preferably more. Ideally decades. Anything shorter than five years is too risky, because of those short-term ups and downs in the market that we regularly see. But in the long term, as the years and decades pass, the risk gets lower and lower, and shares actually become less risky than other forms of investing. Over the long term.

What if you pick the wrong companies, though? It's no good knowing that the stock market will be fine in 20 or 30 years if all of your money has just disappeared faster than the contents of everyone's glass when it's your round. Isn't that a different kind of risk? Yes, it certainly is. But we can even out that risk too. Just as we can beat the short-term risk of the market falling by investing for the long term, we can avoid the risk associated with a single company by spreading our money over a number of companies (somewhere around ten companies is probably a good number). And we can buy companies that are obviously good. Instead of gambling on a small company developing an innovative new kind of portable toilet, we'd be safer relying on, say, a major bank still to be operating well into the next century. If you simply put your money into the ten biggest companies in the UK, the chances are you would do very well. And with pretty low risk too.

Many investments made by private investors do go horribly wrong though, and, more often than not, this is caused by buying a company for the wrong reason – the 'hot tip' approach.

The tip could come from a friend, colleague, a newspaper or even some bloke you bumped into in the newsagent's. The fact is that an awful lot of shares are bought because people have simply 'heard' that they are a good investment. Sometimes tips can go fine, but more often than not they end in tears. It's a bit like playing darts blindfold with someone behind you going, 'Left a bit, right a bit, throw!' So, find out about the companies you are investing in, and only buy ones that you know and can understand. No investment is ever 100 per cent risk-free, but by doing just a little research, the risks can be minimized and great gains enjoyed.

The dartboard experiment

After H+G Investments had been going for a year or so, one of the members made a particularly flippant comment at a meeting. It was just designed as a throw-away line, but it stayed with us for a long time. 'You stand as much chance,' he said, 'of making money in the stock market by doing all this research as by throwing a dart in the share price pages of the *Financial Times*.' Now, another member, who does a lot of research on his own and for the club, took exception to this comment. So a challenge was born. The gauntlet was down! We'll call our two heroes Eric and Jim (for they are modest, and would not take kindly to fame). Eric got a copy of the *FT*. He didn't get any darts, because his mum won't let him play with sharp things, but a blindfold and a finger were enough to pick ten companies. Meanwhile, Jim was scouring his records looking for ten companies that he would choose to invest in at that moment. The rules were simple. The challenge would last one year. A hypothetical £1000 would be invested into each of the ten companies selected by the participants, and the competition would be monitored monthly at the club meetings.

After one month, Jim, with the actively selected portfolio, was well in the lead. Eric said he really didn't expect to win anyway and that it was just a casual comment designed to stimulate discussion (but losers always talk like that, don't they?). Jim's delight was short lived, however, as in Month 2 one of Eric's randomly selected companies was the target of a take-over bid. Another, an extremely dodgy foreign cheese exploration company, actually struck a rich blue vein (or maybe it was kryptonite they were after, not that it matters) and their share price quadrupled. Well, that was it – game over, more or less. Jim never recovered the lost ground and after a year Eric was the competition winner with an overall gain of 24 per cent, while Jim's portfolio struggled to break even.

So, did Eric prove a point? That depends on when the shares would have actually been sold. After one year, which is a very short time to a Fool, then yes, he might have proved something. But investment in shares should be for the long term. Although the experiment officially ended after one year, you may be interested to know that, three years on, Eric's dartboard portfolio shows a gain of approximately 50 per cent, but Jim's actively selected portfolio is up around 125 per cent.

But I don't like roller-coasters

Most stock market risks are associated with short-term price movements, but that risk only turns into real losses if the investor chooses to panic and sell as a result. There is a big difference between short-term price fluctuations and long-term gains or losses (and there are no apologies for repeating that phrase 'long term' all the time. It really is the most important one you're likely to see here. You'll hear it many more times before the end of the book). The first, short-term fluctuations, is really something known as volatility, and the second reflects the genuine risk that your investment faces. Over the long term (there we go again), volatility may not change, but real risk will diminish as the years go by.

Risk is conquered by knowledge, so where is such knowledge to be gained? There's the company report of course, telling you what the company does. But wouldn't it be nice to discuss it with other people to see what they think too – not just your investment club mates, but all those others out there in the big wide world. Enter the Internet. The Motley Fool has many followers who like nothing better than talking about their favourite companies, and the Fool's message boards are where they do it. Lots of companies have their own, dedicated message boards too, and yours might be amongst them. But don't take anyone's opinion as any more authoritative than that bloke down the pub, or that taxi driver you listened to last week, though. Listen, learn, and make up your own mind.

A common message posted on the Fool message boards goes something like this: 'Been watching Scruttock's Piano Scrapers today – price down 10p – anyone know why?'

There may be a valid reason, but the answer is probably simply 'because that's what shares do'. Share prices go up and down. There is a terrific story, probably apocryphal, about John Pierpont Morgan, the renowned American investment banker, financier and art collector, and a visiter to a New York hotel. He gets into the lift alone, and is recognized by the attendant. Never being one to miss an opportunity, the attendant summons up his courage to ask the great man, 'What do you think the market will do today, sir?' 'Fluctuate, my boy, fluctuate!' comes the reply. This is, of course, exactly what share prices do, and sometimes with great short-term volatility.

A private investor might look in a newspaper at share prices and might see the following;

Company	Closing price	Change
Thrapplewaite Nose Flutes	563p	+3p

So Thrapplewaite Nose Flutes have closed the day at £5.63 per share, then – up 3p on the day.

Now that does not look like a particularly big change – only 3p on a £5.60 share. What is not known, though, is that Thrapplewaite may have been as high as £6.00 and then fallen, or it may have been as low as £5.00 and recovered. Either way, a lot of investors would probably have fifty fits if they watched the actual 'intra-day movements' of their shares – watching the real prices as they change throughout the day. Modern-day technology makes this possible using the Internet, of course, but intra-day and day-to-day price changes mean little to long-term Fools. It can be fun, though, and it is a rare investor who can actually switch off and not watch those prices at all. Just remain unemotional and don't act on them rashly, and always remember those excellent words of advice from *The Hitchhikers Guide to the Galaxy* – Don't Panic.

Are there still any doubters out there who want to keep their money in the bank now? Think about this: if you are content to leave your money in a deposit account and earn a poor rate of interest, then why not consider buying shares in that very same bank? Instead of interest you would receive dividends twice a year (your income) and you have the added bonus of hopefully watching the share price rise. Over the last ten years, you would have got a much better return from bank shares than any savings account would have netted you.

3

Why an investment club?

To associate with other like-minded people in small, purposeful groups is for the great majority of men and women a source of profound psychological satisfaction.
Aldous Huxley

Who hasn't heard a story of a private investment going bad, of a 'dabble' on the stock market ending in poverty and tears? Let's face it, we all have, haven't we? Many people have been discouraged from investing in the stock market because of such horror stories, stories of lots and lots of money being lost. But such tragedies happen for two simple reasons. Greed and Ignorance. Basing an investment decision on an overwhelming desire to get rich quick, or buying a company that you know nothing about simply on a tip, isn't investing. It is gambling.

But the fact remains that many people are frightened of the stock market, mainly because they do not understand how it works and do not know of safe and effective – Foolish – ways of investing. Many also do not believe they have enough money to invest. Pooling resources (both cerebral and financial) via an investment club is an ideal way around these problems.

There are always wealthy private investors, those with hundreds of thousands stashed away, who will not see the point of investment clubs. 'You can never get enough to make it worth investing,' they will say. But they're wrong. It soon adds up, and the merry dance of compounding over decades can make for a very happy retirement. And detractors also miss that other vital point – the power that comes from the pooling of knowledge and the sharing of the research workload.

Let's look at the early progress of the H+G Investment Club, then, to see these benefits in action.

In the land of the blind, the one-eyed man is king

At the time of H+G's inaugural meeting, the only actual investing experience any of the members had were those two dodgy deals, Millwall FC and Sycamore Holdings, that had been unmitigated disasters. And both of those made by the soon-to-be treasurer of the club, too. Nobody else had any experience, though, so anything was better than nothing, and burnt fingers can teach a pretty good lesson.

Looking back now, what a strange scene that must

have been – someone who had seen his own shares plummet now trying to convince his friends that starting an investment club was a good idea! Of all the people in the room, it might have been expected that at least one had had a quick 'dabble' at some time or other. But no. So it was, then, that the man with the one eye, the man whose idea this all was, had been chosen to lead. And what were the topics of discussion that fateful day? What did that bunch of naïve but aspiring investors talk about? What would happen should our shares double within a month of buying them, that was it. And if we pumped all of our money into the same company, month after month, could we eventually launch a take-over bid? Ah, the stuff that dreams are made of!

The first three meetings were very ordinary, with just the formalities of setting up and running the club being discussed. We had used the standard constitution, rules and agenda found in the ProShare manual, and, as we had insufficient money to invest, there was little or no discussion about specific companies. The members had been pretty keen to learn, though, to understand what makes companies tick, and what all those numbers and funny ratios that people talk about mean. By Month 4 there was enough money in the kitty to make an investment. We meant business now. This was seriously exciting stuff – after all, that was what the club was there for. The club had £1000 to invest, but what should be done with it? Should it all go on one company, or be split between several to spread the risk? We went for the latter and chose three different companies. The selected few that day were a small company called Hobson (who have since been taken over), Marks & Spencer, and Granada, and the princely sum of £300 was invested in each. Charges and stamp duty took up a chunk of the remaining £100. That £300 in each company wasn't the most cost-effective way of controlling charges, of course, but the club was just starting, and it spread the initial risk and gave members more than one company to keep an eye on. Percentages are percentages, regardless of the size of the holding, and we did very well out of those original three shares, making about 30 per cent on each one in quite a short space of time. We were not short-termers, but it was a nice start.

After six months, a new member joined. He was a successful private investor in his own right. At last! A bit of experience! We had done pretty well using our 'gut-feeling' technique, and we had learned quite a bit about the workings of the market already (it doesn't take long), but having someone there who knew most, if not all, of the answers was a massive bonus. Like most clubs, our membership is quite diverse and we all come from different walks of life. We have found that as you pick up knowledge about the market, you learn to apply that to your own industry or profession in ways you could not do beforehand. This educational side is the real beauty of investment clubs. Of the current twenty members of H+G, thirteen have gone on to own shares themselves as private investors. That is thirteen more people taking greater control over their financial futures.

'I don't have enough money to invest in the stock market'

The minimum amount you need for a single share purchase (to minimize dealing costs) varies from around £250 to around £1000, depending on your broker, and it can take an individual investor quite some time to save such an amount. Investing through a club, though, means that the members only need to accumulate this amount between them.

With a modest monthly subscription of, say, £25 per month, that can be achieved pretty quickly. Most of us in the UK can afford that kind of outlay – it is for our future livelihood, after all. And over the decades, it can add up to a princely sum.

Let's illustrate this with an example. The average stock market rise over the last 20 years has been about 15 per cent per year, and a little over 12 per cent per year since 1919. If you have 20 members in a club, all contributing £25 per month, the monthly subscriptions would add up to £6000 per year. Sounds a lot already, doesn't it? Let's assume zero growth in Year 1 with less than average growth of 10 per cent in Year 2. The whole value of the fund would be

£12,900. If 10 per cent could be achieved year on year (which is not at all spectacular by stock market standards), then after ten years the fund would be worth £100,000.

If the recent average growth of 15 per cent is matched, after ten years the fund will be worth over £155,000 – 55 per cent more than you'd get from a 10 per cent return per year. And, if you can manage the 20 per cent that the Motley Fool's Beating the Footsie strategy is aiming for, then after ten years there will be nearly £200,000 in the pot. And all for just £25 per month!

Oooh . . . too risky!

The fact is that many people still perceive investing in the stock market as too risky. By joining (or starting) an investment club, all the risks are shared. If the club's portfolio is reasonably diverse, then you would have to be incredibly unlucky to lose all of your money. The only dangers lie in putting all of the club's eggs in one basket – investing in only one company, or sticking to just one sector (like dodgy foreign mining stocks that contain the word 'resources' somewhere in the company name), for example, and that's far less likely to happen with a club than with an individual investor. That's not to say that investments with different degrees of risk shouldn't be made, though. No, that can lead to a balanced portfolio, with some higher risk purchases being expected to make better returns. As well as calculated risk, the other kind of risk that can also be minimized is the risk of making a bum decision. We will all make them, from time to time, but it hurts less if it is shared. Let's illustrate this with a story. Are you sitting comfortably? Then let's begin . . .

About a year after H+G started, we decided that investing mainly in 'safe' stocks was a bit boring. We weren't losing any money, but we weren't making a great deal either. A story in a newspaper about a Bolivian mining company called Pan Andean Resources (yep, the 'resources' strategy), made us sit up and take notice. The shares were high risk, the paper said, but they had a large drilling partner and were looking for oil in an exploratory block in Bolivia. If they struck oil, the shares could rocket (very emotive word, that) from their current price of about 16p per share. We had a spare £200 that month and decided to sling it Pan Andean's way. We paid 17.5p per share, but within just a couple of weeks they had dropped down to 12.5p each. But we really weren't that bothered, because the entire investment was only costing each member a maximum of £10. After a few weeks, though, the price began to pick up and move steadily upwards. It reached 60p. Good news was followed by more good news, and then Pan Andean announced they would be releasing a drilling report on the block. The share went up to over £1. The report came out and was brilliantly worded, so much so that it fooled everyone, even the 'Wise' City analysts. The key phrase went something like *'and the prospects look excellent for the remaining wells in the block'*. Fantastic news, surely! Up to £1.40 went the share price! The well report was due out imminently, and the City waited with bated breath. It all went horribly wrong, though, when someone telephoned the company's partner in Bolivia and asked if oil had actually been found. They were told the well was dry, and once the news leaked out the price collapsed to 40p or so. The key piece in the report, of course, was that there was no mention at all about the well *actually* being drilled, only about the *remaining* wells in the block! Pan Andean have never recovered from that, and the shares subsequently reached an all-time low of 6.5p. There is a lesson to be learned here (apart from the obvious ones about not investing in penny shares, not making your decisions based on newspaper tips, avoiding speculative gambles, and always paying careful attention to all the news). And that lesson is that a mistake made by an investment club will hurt individuals' pockets a lot less than a mistake made by an individual investor. Investment clubs are a fine place to stretch one's wings as a fledgling investor.

How to make your Publican really happy

An investment club meeting is a social event too. There are clubs that meet in members' homes, and others that hold their meetings across a table in a restaurant. But most clubs meet in pubs, and this is especially good if you know of a pub with a separate area or room where the meeting can take place in relative privacy.

H+G's pub is a small one, the Horse and Groom in Rochford, Essex. Now, the club's members are not just a bunch of drunken oiks (well, not everyone, anyway) but meetings do seem to go better when punctuated by several beer breaks. In fact, one of our largest single investments came after several members had downed a few too many pints of 'Old Speckled Bishop', or some such fiendishly strong ale. Warmed and relaxed was the atmosphere, and several companies were in the hat for discussion that night. All met with a distinct bout of apathy. Except the last one, which happened to be . . . a *pub chain*! That was it, nothing else got a look-in, and the vote to acquire this member of the Alcoholic Beverages Sector was *unanimous*. Never before in the field of investing have so many hands been raised, by so many, so quickly. It's amazing how much bolder the investments become during particularly liquid meetings. And luckily they all seem to have turned out quite well, too.

The social side to club meetings is mainly a chance to have a night out once a month with similar-minded people, who may well be existing friends that you would not see as much of otherwise. Like any other club, other functions can be arranged. H+G has a social secretary who arranges a Christmas bash (normally held in February or March, as it happens – he drinks Old Speckled Bishop too). There'll be other events too, like a summer barbecue, a night out at the dogs, or a day at the races. Anything, in fact, that will help to create new friendships, and that can only be a good thing.

There we have it then, four rock-solid reasons to start or join an investment club:

1) Education, and the sharing of knowledge and effort
2) Sharing the costs and making more regular investments possible
3) Sharing risks and minimizing their effects on individuals
4) Old Speckled Bishop

4

How does an investment club work?

The freedom to make a fortune on the Stock Exchange has been made to sound more alluring than freedom of speech.

John Mortimer

Individual investment clubs and the Motley Fool online community have many features, apart from that of scale, in common. Both depend on a collective, community spirit to continue to exist and to flourish. Below is an excerpt from the Fool's School section of the Motley Fool web site, talking about investment clubs:

What did people who were Fools at heart do before there was a Motley Fool? Well, many of them participated – and still participate – in investment clubs. Investing has long been something that people generally did not discuss amongst themselves. It was perceived as so mysterious and difficult that those without years of training in the City shouldn't try messing with it, lest they lose their entire nest egg in some silly blunder. Most people just closed their eyes and handed over their life savings to the Wise in the Square Mile, hoping for the best.

Except for a small but growing band of merry investors, that is. These exceptions to the rule were often members of investment clubs. They met regularly to discuss investing in general and various specific shares. They pooled their money and plunged into the market. They took control of their own finances and did it . . . together. In many ways, investment clubs have been a precursor to Fooldom.

Indeed, the Motley Fool has been called 'the world's largest investment club'. At the core of Foolishness is community. Readers across the land share thoughts, asking and answering questions in message boards, chats, and featured articles. Communities of Rentokil investors bat around opinions on the future of pest control. People interested in Marks and Spencer discuss how fast the company can grow and whether the share is currently a good buy. Most of this 'give and take' occurs electronically in Fooldom. But starting now, we're taking a huge step backward toward the time-tested, rewarding tradition of investment clubs. Our online forum will continue to grow every day. But we're now supplementing it by inviting all of our readers to consider forming or joining investment clubs. Intrigued? Read through the articles in this area and consider whether joining an investment club is something you might want to do. Starting an investment club with friends, associates and pets is an excellent way to learn about shares and investing without having to go it alone.

At all times in your investment club think of yourselves as engaged in a co-operative endeavour, building for the future, and you won't go far wrong.

Your H+G treasurer is now running several more clubs, aimed at providing investors with slightly different approaches. The original is, of course, the best established and it is going to run for a very long time indeed. The second, The Brass Monkey Investment Club, started in May 1996 and has a fixed five-year term. Another one or two clubs will start in the autumn of 1999, also running for five years. This should maximize the benefit from all the clubs, the thinking behind it being as follows:

a) The H+G is a kind of pension plan for its members. It will be a very long-term club, going on for decades, so members can use it, at least in part, to help provide for their retirement.
b) With the five-year clubs, there will be one 'maturing' every 2.5 years, and a lump sum will be returned to each member. That will pay for a good holiday, a deposit on a car, a good starting pot for further private investing, or whatever. And why five years? Because that's the shortest time that should be considered long enough for Foolish

investing, smoothing out short-term fluctuations.

Investment Club accounting

An investment club is run pretty much like a unit trust (see the Fool's Guide through the Jargon Jungle) for accounting and ownership purposes (though with a bit of Foolish good sense, it should easily outperform the majority of real unit trusts). The investment vehicles that individual members actually buy and sell are called 'units'. This is best illustrated with an example. There are some numbers coming up, but they won't be hard ones. Well, not *very* hard. Honest.

Let us assume that a club starts with 10 members, and each one puts in £100 to begin with. This means that the club's total value is £1000. This total pound value is converted into units of an arbitrary value each – let's say it is convenient to price these at 1 unit = £1. So, there are a total of 1000 units in the club, with each member owning 100 units. Pretty simple sums so far.

Time for the first investment, and the club decides to buy some shares in the Novelty Pasta Company. Conveniently for our sums, the company's share price is £1, so the club buys 1000 shares at £1 each. (We are ignoring dealing charges here, but that is just to simplify the arithmetic. In reality, the total cost of each investment is what counts, so the club would actually get slightly fewer than 1000 Novelty Pasta shares. The numbers, however, are calculated exactly the same way.) After each month, a valuation is carried out by the club treasurer. This is done simply by dividing the total value of the club's assets by the number of units in circulation to obtain a new unit value for that month. Let's see how that is done in our example.

Let's say the Novelty Pasta Company receives a huge order from China for pasta pieces made in the shape of Chairman Mao, for some great Sino-Italian cultural festival. Investors love this, and the share price doubles, to £2. Here's what the accounts will look like at the end of the month.

Value of 1000 Novelty Pasta Company shares @ £2 each	£2000.00
Cash held in bank	£0.00
Value of club assets	£2000.00
Total number of units in club	1000
Unit value for Month 1 = Value of assets divided by number of units	2.00

Every new pound now put into the club by members would buy just half a unit, after the share price rise. If a further £100 was put in by each member, then each would get an additional 50 units, for a total of 150 units each going into the next month. The club will now have a total of 1500 units. We will imagine we do this, then, and invest the new money in the same company, the Novelty Pasta Company (a bit risky, yes, and not something a real club would be likely to do, but it helps to keep the sums simple). This time the £1000 buys 500 shares.

During the next month, the festival is off, and the Chinese pasta order is cancelled, after Italy beats China 15-0 in a World Cup qualifier and, simultaneously, Chairman Mao is cast out of political favour again. And worse, a freak tornado wreaks havoc with the company's durum wheat harvest. Investors desert the company, and the share price drops to just 50p. Let's see the next month's accounts . . .

Value of 1500 Novelty Pasta Company shares @ £0.50 each	£750.00
Cash held in bank	£0.00
Value of club assets in Month 2	£750.00
Total number of units in club	1500
Unit value for Month 2 = Value of assets divided by number of units	0.5

The next £100 invested per member will buy 200 units of 50p each, and this process is repeated each subsequent month. In this simple example, the club's unit price comes out exactly the same as the share price of the Novelty Pasta Company. That's not surprising really, because that is all the club has bought, and we have ignored charges and commissions, and cash that would normally be kept in the bank for club expenses. In reality, when buying different companies, the club's unit price will form a weighted average of all the club's shareholdings (weighted by the number of shares, and the monthly value of each holding), after accounting for expenses.

This system is known, perhaps not surprisingly, as the **Unit Valuation** or **Unit Accounting System** and more comprehensive examples can be found in the ProShare manual, together with examples of other accounting forms and documents.

For a real club, the actual numbers that come out of the calculations will be a fair bit more complex than this example. But fear not! There are at least two commercially available computer programs written specifically for investment clubs, and which reduce the time it takes to do the monthly valuation down to literally just a few minutes. Probably 99 per cent of clubs use a computer for this purpose, but more on computers later.

The legal stuff

The ProShare manual contains a very informative section entitled 'Investment Clubs and the Law' which sets out in some detail the legal requirements for investment clubs. The relevant law applicable is contained in the Companies Act 1985, the Partnership Act 1890 and the Financial Services Act 1986 (although it is possible that the laws may be amended or superseded by future legislation). There is nothing too onerous here, and we won't get bogged down with a lot of legal jargon, but the core rules to remember are as follows . . .

a) The maximum number of members in a club is 20.

b) Every member must be 18 years old or over.
c) Investment clubs cannot advertise their services.

Club Rules and Constitution

Because an investment club is a recognized legal entity, there has to be a set of rules and a proper constitution. Now, before you slam the book down in disgust at the thought of getting embroiled in all this sort of stuff, those nice people from ProShare have prepared a specimen set of rules and a specimen constitution which is to be found in their manual. These pages are designed to be removed, copied and distributed. If your club requires anything different to the sample ProShare rules, the easiest way, by far, of dealing with this is to adopt the rules as they stand and then have a separate schedule showing any changes you decide to make (a bit like the American Constitution and all its amendments, really). You could spend ages typing everything out again, but you have surely got better things to do with your life. Oh, and don't forget that the club rules are there to serve you, not to restrict you, so don't be afraid to change them as you need to! As long as you stay within the law, you can decide to meet every six months at the top of a cliff and only invest in companies beginning with the letter 'P', if you really want to.

The Club Officials

OK, this is where you need a couple of individuals

who are prepared to put in a bit of work for the benefit of the club. To stay legal, a club has to have a chairperson, a secretary and a treasurer. The chairperson's job is, on paper, the easiest of the three, presiding over each and every meeting, calling each item on the agenda and keeping the members in order. Theoretically, it could be the hardest job, because meetings could become very vocal, and after all, money is an emotive subject, but members usually tend to be quite respectful, though.

The club secretary is the one who will record the minutes of each and every meeting, including the obligatory annual Annual General Meeting, and will be responsible for sending each member an agenda for each forthcoming meeting together with the written minutes of the previous meeting. On most occasions, club correspondence will also be dealt with by the secretary. Access to a computer with a decent word processor is therefore a distinct advantage, and probably essential, really.

The Treasurer's job is the most onerous, having to carry out the Unit Valuation System every month, and handling the accounts of all subscriptions, shares bought and sold, interest and dividends received and anything else financial which must all be prepared and reconciled on a monthly basis. Use of a computer makes the treasurer's job immensely easier, though, bringing it down to a couple of hours per month.

The club officials are responsible for the assets of the

club and are elected annually. Remember that the club could not operate without them, and so do try to make their tasks as easy as possible by responding quickly with any information, money or documentation requested. They are unpaid officials, and are carrying out their duties for the benefit of all the members.

No member of the club can charge a fee for their services, although it is quite normal for secretaries to be reimbursed for their expenses, i.e. postage, stationery, phone calls etc.

What about tax?

Famously, Benjamin Franklin said, 'In this world nothing can be said to be certain, except death and taxes.' And, yes, tax is of course payable. Income tax at basic rate will be automatically deducted from any share dividends or credit interest received by the club. It does not take a genius to work out that if the investments are small, then the amount of income tax attributable to each member is very small too. Capital Gains Tax is a different issue, however, and if a member has utilized their CGT allowance for any one year (about £7000 of gains at the moment), then they may incur a tax liability for which they are accountable.

The ProShare manual covers tax in great detail, so we won't repeat all that here. Tax regulations can change, and there are often hidden subtleties, so it pays for your treasurer to check the current situation with your local tax office. Any member who has any doubts or any questions regarding taxation is advised to seek professional advice.

Stockbrokers

In order to deal in shares on the stock market, it is necessary to engage the services of a stockbroker. There are predominantly two types of broker: advisory and execution only. While advisory brokers are willing to talk about market investments and will freely offer opinions on whether a particular share should be bought or sold, they typically charge a lot more for these services. Because they are paid by commission (that is, they are paid not by how much profit you make, but by how often they buy and sell on your behalf), they have more of an incentive to over-trade your account and rack up the charges. Certainly for an investment club, for whom much of the point of the exercise anyway is about learning together, and also for Fools out there who are committed to managing their own money, there is no point in opting for an advisory broker. Better to go for an execution-only broker, which is much cheaper and who simply carries out buying and selling on your instructions. You can find a host of information on execution-only brokers, including charges, in the brokers section on the Motley Fool web site.

Where do you keep the cash?

Obviously, you will want to open a bank or building society account. You need an account that pays a reasonable rate of interest, but which also allows instant access to the club funds. There are initial and ongoing expenses involved, and the easier it is to get to the money, the better. Surprisingly, at the time of writing, not all savings institutions have suitable accounts for investment clubs. There are stockbrokers who offer special deposit accounts for investment clubs, which makes dealing easier, but is more problematic if you need to write cheques. There are, for instance, initial expenses like the ProShare membership fee, and the stockbroker may wish to check the credentials of the club officials. This will usually involve what is known as a status enquiry, and the cost has to be paid by the club, although it is a very small expense and not applicable on every occasion. At the end of the day, the club members have to weigh up the pros and cons of each alternative and decide on what is most convenient for them. As investment clubs get more popular, there will almost certainly be more alternatives and maybe even some specially designated accounts purely for use by clubs.

How do the members pay their subscriptions?

By far the easiest way for members to pay their subscriptions is by standing order. In addition to the monthly subscriptions, members may wish to purchase additional units, if the club rules allow it (and that is entirely up to you, of course). This is known as 'internal brokerage' and it is explained in depth in the

ProShare manual. If you decide to allow it, members can certainly increase their profitability from the club by buying extra units when the value of them is low.

Specimen standing order mandates can usually be provided by your bank. If, however, they are unable to help you, then it is easy to draw one up yourself. Here is a sample that you are welcome to copy and use.

STANDING ORDER MANDATE

To: The Manager (*your bank*) Bank Sort Code____________

(*Address*) ____

____

____

Account name (*your account*) Number

....

Please pay the sum of £ _________ to the ____________________
Investment Club on the _______ of each month. Please use my surname as a reference. Please commence the standing order on _______ (*date*) __________ and continue paying (*until further notice/until* __________________________ */for* ________ *payments*)*

This is a new instruction and supersedes any previous instruction in favour of

____

*delete that which does not apply

5

How do you decide what to buy?

October. This is one of the peculiarly dangerous months to speculate in stocks in. The others are July, January, September, April, November, May, March, June, December, August, and February.
Mark Twain

There are many, many books on investment strategies and share selection techniques, and some are very good. Before we even start talking about any investing techniques, though, let's quickly mention 'The Fool's Guide through the Jargon Jungle', which you'll find at the back of the book. If there are strange words coming up which you don't understand, just flip to the back and the chances are they'll be explained. By the end of this book, if someone asks you if you consider the yield to be good on blue chips at the moment, you won't think that they are talking about a weird sauce on some fancy Icelandic food.

Valuing shares

Right, this is where it starts to get interesting. There are many methods of valuing a company, to decide whether it is a worthwhile investment or not. One of the most important factors is whether you think the company has a good product, a sound business, first-class management and effective marketing. If it does, you may be prepared to pay more for it than if its line of business wasn't so good. In this section, we're going to talk about a simple way of putting a figure on that, the P/E ratio, but before we go on, please answer the following question . . .

> 'Which is better value, 1 litre of Gofast petrol at 63p, or a 500g box of Brekkyflakes costing £1.00?'

Can't say? OK, we'll come back to it later.

Now, try this one . . .

> 'Which is better value, shares in Universal Corsets PLC at 5p each, or Huge Chemicalco PLC at £25?'

Another tough one? OK, we'll come back to that later as well. But remember these two questions.

There are many ways to put a value on shares. The P/E, or price to earnings ratio, is a frequently used measure of share value (though be warned, on its own it doesn't really tell you anything at all). It is found and quoted everywhere and so it is worth spending a little while on it.

Let us look at a large fictional company,

Thrublington Abrasives International, a multinational supplier of industrial abrasives. Thrublington is the largest company in its sector in the world and is perceived by the market as the leader in its field. This is a company which is clearly not going to go bust, and investors may be prepared to pay a bit extra on the share price for the additional security that a company of this size brings (remember how you should expect to pay more for a quality company?). The share price is currently £2, and Thrublington earned 10p per share this year, giving the company a P/E ratio of 20 (simply the share price of 200p divided by the earnings of 10p per share). Easy. Now, let us say that the company releases a statement saying that trading has been excellent and that the analysts who follow the company decide that next year's earnings are now going to be in the region of 15p per share (analysts often get it wrong, though, and the more analysts who join the consensus the better). Because the earnings are forecast to increase by 50 per cent, you might expect the share price to also rise by 50 per cent, up to £3 in order to maintain the P/E ratio of 20.

Now, a much smaller rival, The Luton Grit Company, has shares priced at £1, and has similar earnings of 10p per share. Luton Grit's P/E ratio is therefore only 10 (100p divided by 10p, remember). The company's earnings per share have not increased for three years. Investors would generally be more wary of Luton Grit, because of its lack of earnings growth and its small size, and therefore are not prepared to pay the extra price that Thrublington commands.

So, which share offers better value? If you are looking to buy £1000 worth of shares, then you could afford 500 shares in Thrublington at £2 (or 333 shares at £3 after they have risen). But you could get 1000 shares in Luton Grit, so is that a better investment? Probably not.

Luton Grit have failed to increase earnings for three years, which, in real terms, means that it is not growing as a company and, when you take inflation into account, they are actually shrinking. This is not very good for the long-term growth prospects of the company or its share price. Thrublington, however, is expected to increase earnings by 50 per cent, and if the company could keep that up for a few years, that might produce some really great returns for investors. So, although the P/E is higher, and the price of the share is higher, Thrublington is probably the better investment.

There are of course other methods of share valuation, but that's not really the scope of this book. It is just to give you a feel for one of the most commonly used indicators when talking about shares. Unsurprisingly, the Fool's School at the Motley Fool web site has a lot of guidelines for valuing shares by different methods.

Investment Techniques

If there are many methods of share valuation, there are even more investment techniques. At the Motley Fool, investing solidly for the long term is favoured as the most sure-fire way to increase your wealth over the course of your lifetime. In this section we'll run through a few investment techniques, some Foolish, some not so Foolish. There are, however, certain things you should know and understand otherwise you will not sleep at night.

1) There are only two prices that are important when thinking of your investments – the one at which you buy and the one at which you sell. Further, the price you buy at is only important at the time you buy, and the price you sell at is only important at the time you sell.
2) It is often tempting to take a profit on an investment, but if you have invested in a sound company in which you believe, why not let that company – and your investment – continue to blossom?
3) Do not put all your eggs in one basket.
4) Do not invest money in the stock market if you will need it within five years.
5) Do not invest in things which you are not comfortable with and don't understand.

These points can be illustrated by recalling a discussion with an acquaintance back in October

1998. The market had just 'corrected' itself (that means it had fallen) to the tune of more than 20 per cent in less than three months. Unfortunately, this person had recently invested all of his savings in the stock market, on large FTSE-100 companies that he was familiar with (the FTSE-100 is just a stock market index that tracks the 100 biggest public companies in the UK, by the way). He had just checked his portfolio valuation and it showed a decrease in value of 23 per cent. He couldn't sleep for worrying about all the money he had lost. But had he really lost anything? He needed to ask himself some questions. Had he sold his investments? No, so he had not realized the loss – it was still only on paper. Did he need the money quickly? No again, not for ten years or more. So he wasn't likely to need to sell anything any time soon and take the loss. What he needed to do was to put his portfolio statement away in a drawer and forget it. He had shares in good quality companies, and the stock market would surely recover from the fall. Sure enough, his portfolio has today recovered the losses, and has in fact moved ahead into quite a reasonable profit. That brings us on to another thing we should do when investing. And that is to consider our comfort level associated with keeping all of our money in shares. If we can't stand to see any short-term losses, and are likely to have sleepless nights when the market is falling, then we should put some of the money somewhere with guaranteed safety. That's what this chap subsequently did. He sold about half of his shares and put the proceeds into a building society account. It does not have the same capacity for growth there as it would in the stock market, but he now sleeps soundly at night. So, while we know that the stock market is the best investment vehicle for long-term investors, and has been shown to have beaten all other forms of investment for the best part of a century, it's no good putting all of your money there if it is going to cost you 30 years of panic and sleepless nights. Find your comfort level, and stick with it.

So here are just a few share-picking techniques that you may come across. We'll start with some of the unFoolish ones first:

Chartism / Technical Analysis

Talk about jargon, chartists have got it all. This method is based purely on share price charts. A chartist (or technical analyst, as they are also known) believes that the future price movements of a share can be predicted by analysing previous movements and looking for patterns in share price charts. They look for things with weird and wonderful names, like 'breakout' patterns, 'golden crosses', 'double bottoms' or 'otters' noses'. (Oh, OK, one of them isn't really a chart pattern.) The nature of the underlying business is irrelevant to chartists, and that isn't the way the

Fools like to invest at all. No, Head and Shoulders is for dandruff, and chartism is not a Foolish method for picking shares.

Day Trading

Day trading is really no more than pure gambling on the short-term movement of a share price. Amazingly, there are over 1 million day traders in the US, where dealing costs are quite a bit cheaper. These are people who look for a ½ per cent gain in a share and then get out. They usually end the day the way they start it, with no portfolio, and for them long-term investing means holding shares overnight. This is not a Foolish technique, and definitely not one for an investment club. Just think – you'd need to hold your meetings every hour rather than once a month.

Dartboard

Nah, throwing darts at a *Financial Times* pinned on a dartboard is not a serious suggestion, really. We only mention it here for fun.

Tip Following

The practice of following tips in newspapers, magazines, newsletters and tipsheets, without understanding the reasons behind them, very rarely succeeds. For one thing, there are far too many tips published each week for you to buy them all. And secondly, they are published to sell periodicals, not to make you rich. No, not one for Fools.

And now, on to some more Foolish approaches . . .

Index Trackers

For individuals, this method of investing, which involves buying a type of pooled investment known as an index tracking unit trust, is very Foolish. It requires no brain to follow and yet will beat over 90 per cent of professionally managed investments by simply tracking the stock market index. For many people, this is as far as they will ever want to go on the investment ladder. Investment clubs aren't likely to want to invest this way, though, because, although it is effective, it isn't terribly interesting to talk about at regular investment club meetings, nor does it provide overmuch long-term educational value. You're there to learn about shares. It's worth tracking your club's performance against the stock market index, though, to see how well it is doing.

Beating the Footsie

This is a very Foolish method of investing too, and relies on the fact that the market tends to punish large companies over-harshly when they don't deliver as good a result as expected. This means the share price goes down in the short term, but there is a tendency for it to bounce back up in the longer term, as the true value of the company wins out. The strategy is based on using companies' yields to identify the ones that are being unfairly judged; then buying them, holding on to them for a year and swapping them for the next set. It is an entirely mechanical strategy, and for more information on it, including details of how to do it, have a look at the Motley Fool investment workshop on the Web. Like index trackers, this method may be more suitable for individuals than clubs, as it doesn't involve much activity throughout the year. Having said that, there would be nothing to stop an investment club adopting this approach for part of its portfolio.

Long-term buy and hold

Ah, now this is a good one. Buy quality companies, often well-known ones with strong brand names behind them, and hold on to them for long periods. These are the businesses that are the backbone of the economy and which provide much of the growth of modern Britain. You'll find these types of companies amongst the FTSE-100 list, the list of the 100 largest companies in Britain.

Growth share investing

Growth share investors try to find small companies with outstanding products or services, and for whom they expect there will be an expanding market in the not too distant future. By investing in companies with the capacity to double, treble or quadruple their sales, or even more, there is the possibility of very great profits indeed. Many Fools are engaged on this search and it provides for lots of discussion at investment club meetings. It's riskier than buying large FTSE-100 companies, but investment clubs may well want to put a few smaller, growth companies into their portfolios.

There are going to be relatively few clubs of 10 to 20 people, composed entirely of those with a Foolish outlook on investing. That means there will often be people who want to invest using many of the unFoolish methods we've described here, methods which don't rely on long-term performance, but more on whims or hopes. Well, that's fine, if it is what you want. You're there to enjoy yourselves and learn about other people's points of view. After a while, you may have some members who are chartists, day traders, or whatever, and you can adopt a variety of techniques and styles of investing to suit everyone. David Berger mentioned in the foreword that tolerance and reasonableness were vital to making an investment club a success and so it is. Sod's Law, of course, says that after reading this book you will go and start an investment club which ends up being populated by chartists, day traders and momentum investors, who *crush* the performance of the Fools amongst you, and *blow away* all the long-term principles of the Motley Fool. If that happens, come and tell us about it on the investment clubs message board at the Motley Fool and we'll shut up shop and move to the Bahamas in disgrace! In the meantime, here are some special investing situations . . .

The B/R (Beer/Risk) ratio

Investing through an investment club is somewhat different to investing as an individual. One of the functions of an investment club is to keep its members' interest and make sure everyone enjoys themselves. That means that sometimes you find yourself doing things which are, frankly, unFoolish. Like occasionally investing in penny shares, which are much more likely to go bust than to provide a good return. H+G Investments, for instance, has a 'Boom or Bust' constituent. Every year, generally at the end of a particularly beery meeting (the higher the risk, the more beer we need, you see), we throw the princely sum of £250 at a really dodgy speculative investment, which, if it performs, could put us on the road to riches. All right, it probably won't, but what's the downside? £250, or exactly £12.50 per member per year. That's the maximum we can lose. In the meantime, it's fun and gives us something to talk about at meetings, but only because of the small-risk investment in a high-risk company spread between all the members of an investment club. It's a bit like having £1 on the 500-1 shot in the Grand National once a year.

Limited Life Clubs

Some clubs, like the Brass Monkey Investment Club, have a limited life of five years, at the end of which time they are to be wound up, with all members receiving their share of the profits (hopefully!). This creates a situation entirely unlike that of an individual investor, who is never likely to be committed to winding up their stock market investments entirely at a defined, unchangeable point in the future. As the time approaches for the end of the club, it may become important for the club's assets to be protected. Normally, we would say that if your company's fundamentals are sound, but the price goes down, then there is no point in selling and realizing a loss. Most unFoolish. Just hang on to the company, because if it's a good one, it will come bouncing back. However, as the date for winding up nears, there may not be time for such short-term price movements to work their way through and right themselves. In that case, one way of partially protecting the club's assets for winding-up day may be to apply a stop-loss. This means setting a limit of, say, a 35 per cent decline in share price at which the club will sell to protect its assets.

The danger, of course, is that a trading cost is incurred, and then that the price might indeed bounce back before the time to wind up comes around. That's why the Fool doesn't normally recommend chasing prices in this way and, while in this special case it may be something to consider, for the individual investing for ten, twenty or thirty years hence, it makes no sense at all.

The Last Bit

So, to conclude this chapter, let's go back to the questions we asked earlier:

> 'Which is better value, 1 litre of Gofast petrol at 63p, or a 500g box of Brekkyflakes costing £1.00?'
> 'Which is better value, shares in Universal Corsets PLC at 5p each, or Huge Chemicalco PLC at £25?'

After reading through all that's been written here, do you feel any better equipped to answer those questions? Hopefully not. Because you have decided that you would need far more information before even attempting a wild guess. For instance, how can you compare Gofast petrol with Brekkyflakes? It might be that Brekkyflakes are doing a 'buy one, get one free' offer, which would get you more for your money. But your car wouldn't run on it, would it? You would have to compare Brekkyflakes with Morning Munchies. The same goes for Gofast petrol. The value is excellent if competitors' petrol is 75p per litre, but not so good if the competitors' petrol is only 59p per litre.

As for Universal Corsets and Huge Chemicalco, the fact that you get more shares for your money with one than the other is no measure of value. In fact, with a share price of just 5p, Universal Corsets is a penny share, a high-risk investment in which you stand a good chance of losing the lot. Huge Chemicalco might be the sector leaders, and as such your money is safe. Well, much safer anyway. With them you won't double or even triple your money in the short term, but long term they're likely to provide a steady return.

Remember always to compare like with like, and do your research, Fool, before making any investments. Then, if you are happy and can understand what you are investing in and why, go ahead. Your fellow club members will thank you for your level-headed approach and the clarity you bring to meetings.

6

Will my computer come in handy?

Man is still the most extraordinary computer of all.
John F. Kennedy

The short answer is 'yes', but that's no good for a whole chapter, is it? You want to know exactly *how* and *why* the computer can be used to work for you.

Earlier, you learned the basics of the Unit Valuation System, and how there are at least two commercially available computer programs that coped with the task of valuing the units of the club and also of keeping the club's accounts.

The H+G club has only used one of these, and that is produced by Computer Office Workshops. The version used is called COW4, and is a DOS-based program, with three components;

1) The Unit Valuation System
2) The Club Accounts
3) A Fantasy Share game

There is also a version called COW2000, which runs

under Windows and is Year 2000 compliant. However, COW4 is very reasonably priced, and certainly does the job as far as our club is concerned. The only part of it which is annoying is the fact that all sales, purchases and dividends have to be entered twice, once for the accounts and once for the Unit Valuation System. This increases the chance of error, and with a better design it could surely have been arranged so that you only need to enter things once, surely?

COW4 also has a module which apparently calculates each member's tax liability, although this is rather confusing and far from clear, and the Tax Office don't seem to want to know anyway.

There are people in some clubs who use Quicken (a financial tracking application) and Excel (a spreadsheet program) for these tasks but the two programs are not integrated. In the future, there will doubtless be other software available for investment clubs, so keep those eyes peeled.

Surely my computer can assist me more than that?

Oh yes. Welcome to the age of the online investor. As computers become more and more powerful, and the Internet more pervasive, information is becoming more and more accessible. Access to the Internet is now becoming crucial, as this is an excellent source of data, much of which is invaluable and not available anywhere else. In no particular order, let's look at some of the benefits computers can bring to investment clubs:

Research

Once upon a time, it was pretty difficult for a small private shareholder to get hold of free information about a company, unless it was old hat and out of date. However, the Internet is shrinking the business world. If there is a company that you wish to research, then it may have its own web site. If so, go to it and see what information you can glean. Some companies will allow you to download the latest annual report, totally free of charge. You may discover something about the company of which you were previously unaware and which backs your judgement. You may discover something which makes your toes curl, although to be honest this is unlikely on the company's own site. To find out what individual people think, you can also use the Motley Fool message boards, where you will find individual message boards for many quoted UK companies. On these boards individual investors can post the results of their own research for others to see, and can also note what other investors think. There are also boards on subjects rather than just companies, such as 'investment clubs', for example. Members here ask questions, possibly about the administration of a club, or ask assistance regarding who to use as a banker or a broker, what shares to look at, and so on. Hemmington Scott (www.hemscott.co.uk) runs a web site on which you can access information from about 3000 quoted companies free of charge. New investment sites are springing up all over the place. Many financial software vendors now provide historical data for the last five years as a standard. There are also many online services that, amongst other things, provide free Internet access for an unlimited period, free delayed share prices, and access to reported directors' dealings. For a small monthly charge, many also offer access to real-time prices on the London Stock Exchange, and other subscription services can provide 'hot off the press' news reports. And all this is just for the UK, where information and access really are getting cheaper all the time. The information available free to US investors is mind-blowing.

One popular product, Company REFS, is a publication produced by Hemmington Scott which is published monthly and comes in two volumes, both large and cumbersome. Alternatively, you can get it on CD-ROM and it contains a wealth of financial and other data on UK companies. A monthly subscription is quite expensive, but it is possible to subscribe quarterly. Other very worthy sites to visit for research purposes are Marketeye (www.marketeye.co.uk), Bloomberg(www.bloomberg.co.uk), Moneyworld (www.moneyworld.co.uk) and Electronic Share Information (www.esi.co.uk).

Other web sites

Many investment clubs across the UK now have their own web sites. There are two clubs, one in the UK and one in the US who recently got involved in a trans-atlantic competition. The UK club had a hypothetical amount of money to invest in the US market, and the American club had the same amount to invest in the UK market (the last news was that the UK club were winning hands down!). ProShare also have a good site which contains an awful lot of information regarding investment clubs. Their web site is at www.proshare.org.uk.

An American club, the Wild Capital Investment Club in Columbia, Missouri, has a massive database of investment clubs, mostly American, but there is an international section with many British Clubs listed. You can find them at www.computerland.net/~missouri/investment_club.htm. Most clubs tend to be pretty helpful when it comes to assisting with set-up or administration issues.

As you can gather, these sites are just the tip of the iceberg – there are ZILLIONS of useful web sites that relate specifically to investment or investment clubs – and that's just in the UK! Once you go to access the American stuff, well, it's pretty amazing.

Newspapers

Yes, many of the daily newspapers have Internet versions too. Certainly broadsheets like *The Times*, *Telegraph*, *Guardian* and the *Financial Times*. You have to register with them, but reading the daily paper is generally FREE! The layout of each one has obviously been tailored for the Internet, but broadly speaking the content is the same. It can be hard finding back, issues though, if you miss a day or two.

Online Banking and Stockbroking

Banks are now getting in on the act, and many banks offer banking facilities via the Internet. Some also include free Internet access with the banking package. There are some stockbrokers that offer online dealing facilities too, although none so far that extends the service to investment clubs. It will come, though, just as it has in the United States. Over there, they are a lot more clued up regarding online broking, which is still in its infancy over here. By the time this book is published, however, there will be an increasing number of online brokers in the UK brokerage market, which looks likely to boom. Real-time online broking resolves the issue of getting through in busy times on the telephone to your broker. Sometimes they simply cannot cope with the volume of shares traded and the calls they are receiving.

Before too long, it will surely be possible to trade shares 24 hours a day on any stock market in the world via the Internet. One of the great opportunities which the online environment offers is the possibility to trade in shares abroad, of which one of the most attractive opportunities is in the US. You'll find more on that and how to go about it later.

7

So what happens at a meeting then?

It is my opinion, sir, that this meeting is drunk.
Charles Dickens

Well, let's see what you think might happen at a meeting. Perhaps, if you are a complete novice, and have never attended an investment club meeting before, you imagine a boardroom type table, seated at which would be a load of sombre people wearing glasses and suits, all equipped with calculators, reading the financial pages and talking in jargon!

WRONG! (Apologies if there *is* actually a club that matches the above description.)

Most of the new male members in our club do attend their first meeting wearing a suit, or at least a tie. Not that we've got anything against anyone who wants to come so attired, it's up to them. But it's another indication of how the ordinary person perceives the world of finance. 'I'm going to an investment club meeting, better look smart.' Why? Too long has the finance industry been synonymous with pinstripe suits, bowler hats and briefcases. Unless the venue or the time of the meeting dictates that smart dress be worn, just relax. You'll enjoy it more if you feel comfortable, and besides, unless the other members in the club are also in smart attire, you'll stick out like an eskimo in the desert. And probably feel like one. In our experience, new members have usually shed the jackets and ties by Item 3 on the agenda. As a rule, wear what you are comfortable in.

Club meetings have to stay within the law, which means that minutes must be taken and recorded. This is usually done by the club secretary (don't worry, shorthand is not required) and then he or she will despatch them to the other members together with an agenda for the forthcoming meeting at some point in the month (assuming the meetings are monthly). The treasurer will usually produce the accounts sheets and will distribute these at the meeting, although sometimes they are sent to the members ahead of the meetings. The club's investments are discussed generally, and any proposals for selling existing holdings or purchasing new ones are made and voted on. Any other club business is then discussed.

A club's very first meeting is slightly different, as we shall see later. Just now, let's see how a meeting might be conducted at a fictional club which meets down a local pub (note: the following events have been based on personal experiences, by talking to members of other clubs, and by reading articles and books).

VENUE: The Dog and Duck

SCENE: Eight members are standing at the bar, chatting and telling jokes. The chairman arrives, accompanied by another member.

CHAIRMAN, BARRY: Greetings, all, sorry we're a bit late, only the cab didn't turn up on time and when I did get round to old slowcoach's house *(he nods disapprovingly at the other member, who looks a bit sheepish)*, he wasn't ready! Still, better late than never eh? Who's got the whip?

(Another member acknowledges that he in fact holds the whip, and then proceeds to collect £5 from the two new arrivals. Every member puts this amount into the whip. A round of drinks is purchased, and the members make their way to the meeting place, which is an alcove approximately six feet from the edge of the bar, and definitely within yelling distance.)

BARRY: Right, let's get this show on the road, as they say, meeting opened at 8:45, hands up all those not here *(he says this every month, and the other members still laugh)*. Okey-dokey, all those not here have been marked accordingly, and because there was an extremely good turnout last month, there is more money in the whip to be carried forward, is that right, John? *(John holds the whip)*.

JOHN: Absolutely right, we have £35 carried over, and £50 going in tonight, so it's gonna be a good meeting! *(Chuckles all round)*

BARRY: Excellent, right, I've had some apologies for

absence which I've passed on to the secretary already, so on to the first item on the agenda, the minutes of the last meeting. Did you all get them, and were they a fair reflection of last month's gathering? If not, speak up now, otherwise we shall take them as read and move on . . . *(silence from members)* Right, moving on, for those who remember, were there any matters arising? *(Generally silence, but one member thumbs his copy of the minutes)*

KEN: Did we actually renew our subscription to ProShare?

TREASURER, LAURA: Yes, sent the cheque off myself.

BARRY: Excellent . . . right, anything else? No? OK then, moving swiftly on. . . Secretary's report. Richard?

SECRETARY, RICHARD: Nothing this month, except that someone has sent us a video of a pyramid selling scheme and reckons we should invest in it. I don't and I doubt anyone here will either. I think we should send it back with no postage on it.

GRAHAM: Better still, why don't we record our own video message saying we're not interested and send it back to them? I'm sure we could think of something suitable. *(Knowing smiles all round)*

BARRY: Excellent, I like that idea, we'll organise that. Right, treasurer's report, over to you . . . Mark!

LAURA: Thank you, Barry, right, here is the accounts sheet *(distributes sheet)* and you can see

that we received several dividends which, when added to last month's sale of Old English Pub Company following their profits warning, means that we have £5000-odd in the kitty to spend.
BARRY: Excellent, any questions? No? OK, without further ado let us hammer straight into the Investment Update. Did anyone see anything about our companies last month?
(The meeting turns serious for a few minutes as members report what they have seen or heard about the club's shares in the last month. There is a sudden interruption from a lot of cheering from across the pub where there is a TV screen. Manchester United has just scored in a European Cup match against some foreign team. A few club members enquire of the score and discover they are winning 1-0. After a minute or so, the meeting restarts.)
BARRY: Has anybody else anything to add? No? Good, we'll be home for the highlights at this rate . . . next item . . . Internal brokerage. Does anyone want to buy any more units this month? *(A couple of people dive into their pockets and produce some crumpled notes, and one member writes a cheque)* 'So, that's Tim £25, Bill £25 and Alan £50. Good. New Investments, then.
GRAHAM: I'd like to propose Dixons. I'm working on a refit of their stores at the moment, and talking to some of the staff they seem to think that things look really good for the future.

LAURA: Looking at the IT sector, I think that the millennium bug problem is going to produce a lot of work for specialist IT staff. DCS are major beneficiaries of that, and we already hold them, but a more specialist company is MSB International. They are down to about £3 from a high last year of over £10 and could be worth a shot.

TONY: Based on the fact that Manchester United are winning tonight, and are top of the league and still in the FA Cup, I think we should look at them.

JOHN: I've been looking through the press and the recent results and forecasts for Character Group look terrific. They distribute toys and have licences for lots of Disney and Marvel stuff. I think they had Buzz Lightyear and the other Toy Story merchandise. The shares are about £2.50, up from just over a quid last year. I'd also like to recommend topping up on Card Clear.

BARRY: Anybody else?

ANGELA: I've been reading good things recently about Jarvis, the building company.

JOHN: You may remember that I recommended these to the club about two years ago when they were 94p . . . and they are now over £3.

(John smiles and looks smug. Other members groan. John is renowned for this.)

SHAUN: Mr Chairman, can we minute an 'I-told-you-so-moment', please? *(Laughter from members)*

BARRY: Sounds fair to me. Sorry, Alan, you were

saying.

ANGELA: Yes, I was reading that Jarvis will probably get a massive contract from the government to build thousands of new homes. Might be worth looking at.

BARRY: Before proceeding, I am going to call a beer break, firstly because I'm thirsty, and secondly because it's my job as the chairman. *(Laughter – beer and nibbles are ordered. After about 5 minutes, everyone settles.)* To recap then, Richard, can you read out the proposals please.

RICHARD: Yes, we have Dixons, MSB, Manchester United, Character Group, Card Clear and Jarvis.

BARRY: Well, you've heard the proposals, we have five grand to spend, so let's pick two each and see what happens. *(Barry then goes to each member who in turn names two of the five companies proposed. Richard the secretary is logging the votes.)* So, what are the 'scores-on-the-doors', then?

RICHARD: Dixons have 2, Man. United have 4, MSB have 1, Character Group have 8, Card Clear have 4, and Jarvis 1.

BARRY: So, we have a clear winner in Character Group, and a tie for second place between Card Clear and Manchester United.

LAURA: I would like to propose that as we have £5000, we spend £2000 on Character Group and £1500 each on Man. United and Card Clear.

BARRY: Sounds good to me . . . all those in favour

(all but one member raises their hands) and against *(the one member raises his hand)*. Good. . . carried by a majority of 9-1. Tim, can we ask why you voted against?

TIM: Just to be awkward, really. I like to express a contrary position.

BARRY: Well, that's very commendable, but you've been outvoted anyway. *(Laughter from all)* Next item on the agenda is our social report and the obligatory joke-telling session.

(Tony, the club's social secretary, relays some information about the club's planned Christmas 'do' at the local casino, and then tells an extremely poor joke. Other members chip in, various jokes are told.)

BARRY: Right, all, the final item on the agenda, Any Other Business. Is there any? *(all members silent)* Well then, meeting closed at 10:20. How much left in the whip, John?

JOHN: About £30.

BARRY: Right, that's good for another couple of rounds of beer and nibbles. . .

Meetings can of course be made more serious if so desired. For instance, it may be possible for visits from a local company to be arranged. At the end of the day, members will want to enjoy themselves, but will also want to learn and, hopefully, make money. It is an investment club after all.

8

What happens if it all goes pear shaped?

A real gentleman, even if he loses everything he owns, must show no emotion. Money must be so far beneath a gentleman that it is hardly worth troubling about.
Fyodor Dostoyevsky

As has been made plain, I am the treasurer of a number of investment clubs, and I am pleased to say that they all run pretty smoothly. However, money is a very emotive subject, and there is certainly a lot of scope for friction to exist between members if things don't go to plan. Here are some pitfalls and problems to avoid.

The profit snatcher

Members themselves have to learn how to treat money when it is invested. From the club's point of view, all investments need to be given a chance to perform, and no-one should expect a return from any share within a year, at least, preferably three. Some prospective members think that immense gains will come next year just because the club has performed well in the past. What's that phrase that they love to throw at you when selling financial products? 'Past performance is no guarantee of future performance.' That's true of investment clubs too and anyone who has unreasonable expectations will not only be sorely disappointed, but will be a destabilizing influence.

Then there are the members who want out if the club makes a very quick profit. These people are all too keen to 'take the money and run'. But where will that get anybody? Suppose an investment club has 20 members, and each has put in £500 in subscriptions over an 18-month period. During this time, the club's investments have all performed beyond the wildest expectations of any member, and the portfolio has grown to be worth over £17,000. One member decides that he will take his profit and gives his notice in. The club now has to sell one of the investments in order to pay him off. They might sell the one that will return the biggest profit over the next three years. How are they to know which one to get rid of?

The above example is unfortunately not that uncommon. The other club members have been penalized because someone wants to take their profit.

Stock market investment via an investment club is not for this type of opportunistic person. It is always essential to look at investments with a long-term view. One option is for the club to set a future date when a pay-out of any profits may be made to members. This may stop some members wanting to cash in too early.

The 'Doom and Gloom' Merchant

Equally dangerous from a club perspective is the member who is so pessimistic that each time the price dips he wants to sell. This type of person, and yes, they do exist, is one that would be unpopular in a club environment. Profits should not be snatched and losses should not be realized without good reason and research. The club should decide beforehand in what kind of situations it will sell shares, preferably when the underlying story has changed, and if all club members are aware of this and accept the risks as well as the rewards, then no-one should turn out to be a 'doom and gloom' merchant.

The Fidget

Some members have the best intentions. They take an interest, watch the markets, and it consequently drives them mad that the share they were going to introduce at tomorrow night's meeting has just been the target of a take-over bid and the price has doubled. 'If only we had bought them last month, or even last week,' they muse. 'Surely we can keep some money back so we can buy something mid-month if the opportunity presents itself?' Well, forget it. This is an absolute no-no for any club, and possibly the biggest danger. Let's spell it out: **It is grossly unfair on any one member to give them the responsibility of buying shares in between club meetings in companies that have or have not been discussed by the club, even if they appear to be at**

bargain prices. Such a policy would surely be a recipe for disaster. Can you imagine the problems that would be caused if a club official took it on his own back to buy 1000 shares in some company or other a few days before the meeting, and it all went horribly wrong?

Here's a 'true life' example, which shows both the dangers of this practice and, even more importantly, the great dangers of acting on the basis of rumours or tips, rather than the basis of your own research and concrete information:

I have a friend who lives in the US and who belongs to an investment club over there. He is not the treasurer, but he is one of the three people allowed to trade stocks on the club's behalf with the broker.

He contacted me regarding a company traded on the NASDAQ Exchange called Penn Interconnect, mainly because he thought I might be interested personally and for the clubs that I run. A story had been propagated on the Internet, from a fairly well known source, that this company was about to merge with a rival and that together they would completely corner their particular niche of the market. Even if there was no additional growth then business would more than quadruple overnight. The merger valuation had been put at something ridiculous for this company, something like $75 per share. Prior to this announcement the shares were just $8, and since the story had been released, the price had shot up to $24 and was rising. He was going to get $10,000-worth for his club, but as the price had already increased 300 per cent I persuaded him not to. 'This is an entirely unsubstantiated rumour,' I told him, 'and anyway, shouldn't you get the club's approval first, especially for this kind of short-term profiteering?'

'Strictly speaking, I should, but apparently the likely price it will hit is $75-odd, and there is a long way to go. Still, perhaps you're right,' he replied, through obviously gritted teeth. Anyway, here's what happened to Penn over the next three days.

Day 1 – Shares continue to move rapidly up, to over $100, before closing at about $80. Friend in US club threatening to lynch me.
Day 2 – Penn themselves issue a statement saying that they are aware of the rumour on the Internet and that there is no truth in it. Price drops to $45 but still healthy gains to be made. My name is still mud with my US friend for talking him out of making the investment.
Day 3 – Due to unrelated financial problems, the shares are de-listed from the NASDAQ exchange. These shares now cannot be traded at all. My friend breathes a huge sigh of relief and performs a virtual pat on the back from across the Atlantic.

Yes, don't listen to rumour or hypesters – not everyone out there has your best interests at heart and that even goes for the Motley Fool message boards.

And don't make a trade between meetings if it hasn't been discussed first.

Just imagine the problems he would be having if he had gone out on a limb to buy these shares for the club without discussing it with them first. If the club had decided to buy them, then fair enough, that would have been a club decision, however poor a one that may have been. It is, though, unreasonable for one member to expect to have *carte blanche* in running the show without reference to the other members, and unfair for the other members if one person has ultimate power to do as he likes. The club must make its own investment decisions as a unit and if it does not do so, then it will sooner or later (probably sooner) be finished as a club.

There are some minor exceptions to this rule. It is quite acceptable for the club to meet, make a decision to purchase some shares at a certain price, and give a member the power to purchase them at some point in the next month if they hit that price.

Otherwise, investment decisions must be made at monthly meetings. Any 'fidgety' people who want to duck and dive around the market would be best to adopt these tactics on their own rather than within a club.

The Mouse

I have, in the past, come across timid people who think that £20-£25 per month is too much to put into an investment club. Don't get me wrong – it's not that they cannot afford the money, they just don't feel comfortable putting that amount into a club. Clubs are not for this type of person. £20 is the *absolute minimum* that could be put in and still make the club an interesting proposition for its members. The danger otherwise is that it will take so long to accumulate enough money to buy anything that enthusiasm may well be lost.

So, now we've identified potential problem members, and you've established that none of them apply to you, we can look at other problems and pitfalls that clubs may need to address.

When can members take money out?

A good point and a common problem for many clubs. As we have seen, a member wishing to withdraw funds all of a sudden can force a club to sell investments in order to pay him or her off. For this reason, there need to be some fairly clear guidelines in the rules about withdrawals. If a member does leave, of course, then their entire holding must be realized and the ProShare guide recommends that they should receive their funds within 90 days of giving their notice to leave. Some clubs have a 'no withdrawal' rule and operate for a fixed term, so that all members know exactly when they will receive their money. This eliminates the uncertainty, but at the same time it must be recognized that the winding-up date may not turn out to be the most advantageous time to sell up. As long as the situation is made clear to all members, then most of the problems connected with withdrawals can be avoided.

What happens if a member leaves?

We've touched on this already, but if a member wants to leave then here is the procedure.

Firstly, they should give written notice to the club expressing their desire to leave. The actual reason is of little importance, so don't turn it into a big thing. They may be somewhat embarrassed by your asking anyway, and they may have other problems that they do not wish to be made public.

The club, then, has to decide how to raise the money to pay them off. Unless the member's holding is quite small, this will probably involve selling some stock. Which stock to sell is of course open to discussion at the time.

In order to give the club the maximum flexibility, it is recommended that the member leaving should expect to receive their money within 90 days. This effectively gives the club three months in which to deal with the issue of raising enough money to pay off the member or members concerned. Whether the club makes the member wait three months or not is up to them, but in my experience if a member has left it is usually because they have needed the money to cope with some unforeseen occurrence. We have always tried to get money to departing members as soon as possible.

What if a member dies?

It hasn't happened in any of the clubs that I am in yet, but it is obviously bound to happen at some point to someone. And, by a curious twist of fate and happenstance, my career as a Trust and Estate Practitioner, which has me dealing with the estates of deceased people on a daily basis, leaves me fairly qualified to advise on this particular point. So this is what you should do, *officially:*

a) Ask for a copy of the death certificate.
b) Freeze the deceased member's holding.
c) When the Grant of Probate is received, ask for a copy, which should be registered in the club records.
d) The holding can then be realized and a cheque sent to the personal representatives of the deceased member.

However, if this unfortunate event occurs, then you do not really want to put your friend's or colleague's family through these procedures, which are reserved for more inflexible and less understanding institutions. So here is what you *actually* do:

a) Express deep sorrow and regret, and find out who

is dealing with the estate.

b) Ask what is to happen to the money, as it is part of the person's estate and has to be dealt with according to the terms of the will, if there is one, or under the law of intestacy if there isn't (which more or less means it will go to the next of kin).
c) Treat it in the same way as if the member were leaving, and try to raise the money as quickly as possible.
d) Send a cheque to wherever it needs to go.

Hopefully, you will never need to deal with this eventuality.

How do you wind the club up?

Sooner or later, no matter how successful, all things have to come to an end. This may be because the club has come to the end of its fixed term, or it may be because the members have decided that it has run its course. *(Note: the ProShare manual offers guidance as to how members can elect to dissolve the club.)*

At this time, all the investments need to be turned into cash. Please note that the winding up of a club does not happen overnight. It may take a few months to collect all of the assets (outstanding dividends, etc.) and members should be made aware of this fact. Then it simply remains for the treasurer to prepare a final valuation based on the total amount of cash realized, and distribute this between the members according to how many units they hold. Easy!

We have attempted to highlight the major problems faced by investment clubs, although there are others, such as arguments between members, unscrupulous and manipulative members, and even fraud, at the extreme. If any crime is committed, then that is of course a police matter. But as for members' individual behaviour, come on, we're all adults and are expected to behave accordingly. There is no room for petty disputes and squabbles within a club.

9

Suppose the members get bored?

Boredom is just the reverse side of fascination: both depend on being outside rather than inside a situation, and one leads to the other.
Susan Sontag

Many people perceive the financial world as boring. These are people who have absolutely no interest in the stock market and who freely admit the same. In fact, they probably take no interest in money at all, except perhaps spending it. They are quite happy to work hard for their money, and it never dawns on them that they could make their money work hard for them.

The jargon used does not help, but hopefully this book will have clarified at least some of the more common terms in everyday usage. You, dear reader, by getting this far in the book, have a distinct advantage over your compatriots who perhaps think that reading the financial pages of the paper is an occupation reserved for the extremely wealthy, the extremely old, or the extremely boring.

When people elect to join an investment club, it may be for a variety of reasons. It is unlikely to be purely to make money. The social side may particularly appeal, or it may be the prospect of learning about the workings of the market that makes the idea so attractive. After all, so many people *know* that they should be making adequate provision for their retirement, but apart from perhaps a company pension scheme or a private pension, few are actually doing it. So, why do members sometimes get bored?

There are many reasons why a member's interest can start to wane, but from personal experience, it is generally due to a lack of comprehension of what is going on at the meetings. Everyone learns at a different rate, and whilst some members can pretty easily grasp P/E ratios and the like, others may not catch on quite as quickly. If they are then unfortunate enough to miss a meeting or two, then the next time they attend they might struggle to understand something else. They may not wish to ask a question which might make them appear daft, and so they will generally keep quiet and listen, hoping that the situation will clarify itself. If it doesn't, then they may lose interest because they can't understand what is being discussed, and so will become bored. They may then elect not to attend future meetings for fear of being further embarrassed. This is one reason why any sort of compulsory attendance rule is a bad idea, as it doesn't seem right to force people into coming along to meetings if they feel uncomfortable in doing so.

If you think some members are getting bored, or if you are, then get the club officials to look at the format of the meetings. Are they too dry? Is too much jargon bandied about? Are they social enough? Can the club look at ways of livening things up?

Here are a few of the things that can be done to maintain members' interest:

Jokes

We have a compulsory joke-telling session in one of the clubs. This comes towards the end of the meeting and is generally very popular. We have a social secretary whose job it is to get the ball rolling, but after that it's a free-for-all, and the quality of the jokes depends on the members in attendance.

On the Motley Fool web site there is a message board called Jokers Corner, which is living proof that you can be interested in shares *and* possess a sense of humour. The rules for the board are that all jokes must be clean and inoffensive; a good rule of thumb is that if you feel comfortable telling the joke to your mum, then it's probably OK. It would seem rude at this point to leave without a few jokes, straight from the boards . . .

> *A white horse strolls into a pub. At the counter the barman looks at him and says 'Well, well, what a coincidence, our pub is named after you!' The horse*

looks at him in amazement and says 'What . . . Eric?'
A young executive was leaving the office one evening when he found the Chief Executive standing in front of a shredder with a piece of paper in his hand.
'Listen,' said the CE, 'this is important and my assistant has left. Can you make this thing work?'
'Certainly,' said the young man, flattered that he had been asked for help. He turned the machine on, inserted the paper and pressed the start button.
'Excellent! Excellent!' said the CE as his paper disappeared inside the machine. 'I need two copies of that.'

Did you hear about the bloke the police found dead inside an ice cream van? He was lying there stone cold, covered in cream, strawberry sauce and hundreds and thousands. Police believe that he had topped himself!

And finally . . .
Nelson Mandela is at home watching TV when there is a knock at the door. A Japanese delivery man is clutching a clipboard, pointing to a truck full of car exhausts in the driveway and yelling: 'You sign, you sign.'

The bewildered president will do no such thing and slams the door. The next day, the man is back, waving a clipboard under the great man's nose, gesturing to a truckload of brake pads and insisting: 'You sign, you sign.'

Nelson gets rid of the man again, but next day he's back with two truckloads of car parts, once again insisting that the president sign for the goods.

Mandela loses his temper and yells: 'Look, I don't want these. Do you understand? You must have the wrong address.'

Puzzled, the Japanese man consults his clipboard and asks: 'You not Nissan Main dealer?'

Sorry.

Social Events

Apart from telling jokes, our social secretary also has the onerous task of arranging our Christmas do, and we often have a summer barbecue in a kindly member's garden. Don't forget, it's a club, and there is no reason why you should not have separate social events just like any other club. One year we went ten-pin bowling, and then on to an Italian restaurant. Another year, we went for the meal first and then trudged off to the local casino, where we had a competition to see who could make the most money in two hours with a stake of just £25. Needless to say, there were not many people still left in at the end, which proves what a terrific business casinos are for their owners. But if arranging additional functions isn't really your thing, then don't worry. Just doing very simple things can go a long way. The Brass Monkey Investment Club held the December meeting one year in a local Chinese restaurant instead of the pub where we normally meet, which was very successful. The possibilities are endless and it just depends how far you want to go.

Fantasy Share Competitions

Many clubs use this type of game to spice up the meetings themselves. It basically consists of each member choosing a share (or a number of shares) and seeing who has made the highest gain over the month. If a small entry fee was charged, then this could perhaps be used as a cash prize, or, alternatively, to purchase a bottle of something to give to the monthly winner. Some could be held back to be used as a bigger prize for the overall winner after a year.

The *Mail on Sunday* and the *Mirror* both currently run share competitions which, at the time of writing, are free to enter for all ProShare-registered investment clubs, and there are some substantial monthly cash prizes on offer. Members could take it in turn to research and nominate the share for the competition.

Again, there are many possibilities here. The computer software we use, COW4, comes with a built-in Fantasy Share game which is used by many clubs. There is another benefit to playing a game like this: members get used to looking up share prices on a regular basis, and watching the same companies frequently may help members understand why share prices move.

Making all the members feel part of the club

Most types of club rely on just a few members for all the administrative issues, and investment clubs are no exception. However, it is important that one member who appears to know more than the others should not be allowed to bulldoze others into decisions. It is all too easy for members who perhaps are less knowledgeable about a company or companies to sit there and agree with the member who has done the research, but people sometimes can be blind to the facts if they really favour the company. Let's look at a company, Character Group, to cite a particular, and recent, example.

Character Group (previously called Toy Options) is in the toy distribution and character licensing business. You may have read about them in the national press and we already talked about them in one of the example investment club meetings in an earlier chapter; they had the licences to distribute the Spice Girl dolls, and also the Buzz Lightyear and Woody toys from *Toy Story*. Over the last few years they have also acquired companies that have various licences permitting distribution of Disney and Marvel Comics characters in various parts of the world. Character Group's results have been fantastic to say the least, and they are no doubt an interesting investment prospect.

Now, the company's interim results were due to be released on 1 June 1999. At the Annual General Meeting in January 1999, it was announced that the company would have some licensing rights for various products relating to *Star Wars – Episode 1: The Phantom Menace*, the Lucas blockbuster strongly tipped to break all records. However, these licences did not extend to the actual action figures, which are by far the best-selling toy merchandise. Not to worry, the prospects still looked good.

In the weeks leading up to the interims, various news stories and press statements were released, one of which related to the production of *Star Wars* money boxes, retailing at about £40 each. There were three in the series, and if they were all collected, then they would interact together. Very clever indeed.

H+G Investments were holders of the stock, and when this information was excitedly relayed to the club at the monthly meeting, it was met with general approval, with the exception of one member, who is normally quite quiet, and who doesn't say much. When he was asked his opinion of the deal, he said that he thought the money boxes were extremely expensive, and that he wouldn't consider paying out £120 for a set of them just so they could 'interact', whatever that was. His views had nothing to do with the company, the earnings, profits or whatever; it was just straightforward common sense and the other club members had to agree. We liked the company so much, we had overlooked something very basic and simple. The words 'wood' and 'trees' spring to mind. Anyway, this spurred us to look at the company a little more closely, and we discovered that a) a contract with a major client had been lost, and b) in mid-May 1999 the company had re-released the story about the licences for the various *Star Wars* products – but not the action figures – and we could have been forgiven for thinking it was breaking news. We had to think about why they would do such a thing, and wondered if they were trying to fill a news gap when there really was no particular good news at all. There was certainly no positive news about first half earnings prospects to be seen, and the interim results were due to be reported soon.

This was an interesting perspective, which we wouldn't otherwise have appreciated, and although it was the short term that was giving us cause for concern, we remained quite optimistic about the long term for Character Group. Sure enough, the interim results were not as good as expected, and the share price consequently dropped by about 25 per cent.

Subject to their agreement, it may be an idea to select different members to keep an eye on one or two shares and to report their findings at the next meeting. It depends on how much they want to get involved, but an active member is generally a happy member.

Take breaks

It certainly doesn't do any harm to break off from the meeting for drinks, sandwiches, or even just a chat. Upon resumption, the brain is refreshed and the meeting will probably run more smoothly.

Make sure only one meeting is in progress
There is nothing more disheartening for a member who is telling the club about his research into a company to find that two or three members are not listening, or are discussing something completely separate. Apart from being rude, the speaking member may be less inclined to share information in the future and could lose interest in the club himself. The chairman should usually bring meetings to order, but if you are a speaker, then make sure that your voice can be heard by all, and if someone else is speaking, then afford them the courtesy of listening to what they say! You never know, it could be important.

In the past couple of years, the number of clubs in the UK has increased almost ten-fold to 3300. In the US, there are over 50,000 investment clubs, and it is estimated that 1.5 million people are members of clubs in 23 different countries. However, it is sad to say that a good many clubs will not make it past their first three years, and a lot of the failures are down to the lack of interest shown by the members.

We have highlighted several ways in which interest can be maintained, although there must be many others too. However, to maintain interest in your club, just use some basic human psychology: don't force a member to do something they do not wish to do, treat all with respect, keep things lively and you will be fostering a thriving and enjoyable investment club which will not only educate, but hopefully enrich and amuse as well, which also happens to be the three basic aims of the Motley Fool.

10

Can the club invest abroad?

A man's feet must be planted in his country, but his eyes should survey the world.
George Santayana

Another way of putting this question is 'Would you want to consider investing anywhere else other than in good old Great Britain?'

To put it mildly, yes you would.

Now, don't take that the wrong way – British inventors have given the world many truly wonderful and earth-shattering innovations (including the computer, believe it or not), and we've got some excellent companies in the UK. But it is a fact that 39 of the top 50 worldwide brands (in order of financial value) were associated with American companies and absolutely none were associated with UK companies (information taken from *Hoover's Handbook of World Business*). These are all brands we know and use in our daily lives and which have worldwide reach.

Couple this with the fact that the US market is

currently the largest market in the world, and that the London market tends to mirror what happens in the US, and you have a very good reason to consider investing in the US.

Once upon a time, investing in foreign markets was a pursuit best left to the professionals and the institutions. A newspaper article as recently as 1997 actively discouraged foreign, and especially US, investing. 'The time difference would kill the deal,' it said, 'as bad news would be heard across the Atlantic first, and the poor UK investor would be left to pick up the pieces.'

Firstly, that kind of short-term approach to the markets is not the way any Fool, let alone an investment club, should be investing, and secondly that is no longer the case. This is one of the main areas where the Internet comes into its own. The Internet has so shrunk the world that there is absolutely no time difference whatsoever between someone in New York and someone in London – including a private investor – receiving the same information.

That last statement is quite mind-boggling, and would have been inconceivable just a few short years ago, so go back and read it again, just once more.

Any company, whether they be American, French, Australian, or whatever, can release information to the market that is accessible to anyone on the Internet at exactly the same time, no matter where they happen to be on the planet. (Whether they choose to do so or not is another question entirely and, worldwide, US companies are the most open in this form of disclosure. UK companies lag far behind.)

This means that there is absolutely no time advantage for someone in New York as compared to someone in London in whatever market they are trading; there is a level playing field for all.

It is only when you start to contemplate the revolutionary nature of what is not actually a terribly sophisticated technology that you begin to appreciate why Internet stocks are all the rage at the moment (at the time of writing), and why no-one appears to be able to put a proper value on these companies. In the history of the world it seems fair to say there has never been any other phenomenon which has had the potential to influence the lives of so many people in such a short time and has offered so many novel business possibilities.

So, how can the Internet help you and your club to invest abroad?

Well, first of all, foreign investing is not made particularly easy for you by the majority of UK stockbrokers. The dealing charges are astronomical, many low cost, execution-only brokers will not deal in foreign stocks anyway, and there tends to be a minimum trade requirement of at least 100 shares. This doesn't sound too bad until you learn that the majority of American stocks are priced upwards of $30 per share, and so you are looking at a minimum investment of $3000 (approx. £2000). Many great

American companies, like McDonald's, Microsoft, or Pepsi, have share prices far in excess of this figure, even into the hundreds of dollars. Therefore the minimum investment through UK brokers, with a commission charge based on a percentage of the trade, will cost an arm and a leg. Most clubs could not afford such deals.

However, using the Internet, you can now open an account with an online broker that will give you real-time trading on the US stockmarket, for a flat-rate fee of . . . wait for it . . . are you ready for this? Anywhere from $20 down to $10 or even less per trade. Yes, that's **$10** per trade. Approximately £6.25. And this is instant online dealing, over the Internet. There are now many companies offering this kind of deal, some of whom will open accounts for UK residents. You apply over the Internet, but they send the forms to you and they have to be returned by normal post (or snail mail, as it is affectionately known). Money has to be sent to your US broking account by a bank transfer, and then away you go. Many also offer special trading accounts for investment clubs. It really is that simple.

Here it's worth quoting directly from the Motley Fool web site about buying shares in the US market. As of the summer of 1999, one company has set up a UK-based online brokerage to deal in US shares and others will surely follow. As the following article (by Nigel Roberts) shows, it really isn't all that difficult to set up a US online brokerage account in the US either. On with the show, Nigel . . .

Buying Shares in the US

It really is Foolishly simple.

There you are, sitting at your computer screen, contemplating the long term and trying to work out which share you should buy next. Will it be a FTSE-100 share? Or a FTSE-250 one? Or how about a small cap share? Or even (heaven forbid!) a penny share? But wait. Before you commit yourself, how many of you have thought about buying into an American company and been put off by the perceived complexity of it?

Think again. Buying shares in US companies is in many ways easier and cheaper than buying shares in UK companies. Most people reading this will know that the Motley Fool itself is originally an American innovation. How many, though, will know that of the world's top 50 brands in order of financial value, 39 are associated with American companies and – you've guessed it – none are associated with UK companies? This means that many, many of the companies over there are just as familiar to us, or more so, than our own. Ever heard of Microsoft, Nike, Gillette, Wrigley, Pepsi, Coca-Cola, Johnson and Johnson, Disney? It's hard to imagine that British consumers are much less familiar with the products of these worldwide giants than are their US cousins.

We all know that the US is full of great companies which are worth investigating. Why not check out our sister site at Fool US and see what bountiful information is available on American shares? Having a quick peek will also show you what we are targeting for the Fool UK site in years to come. Never fear, though, the UK site will be developed in a very British manner – after all, we do like to do things our own way on this side of the Atlantic!

So once you have visited Fool US, and have decided that you'd like to take a stake in online bookshop Amazon, at their current stellar valuation, how do you go about doing it?

Well, you could phone up your UK broker and ask them to buy the 'stock' for you (remember, we're talking American now), but you will pay through the nose for the privilege. A typical UK execution-only broker of our acquaintance deals in any overseas securities at a commission of 1.8 per cent, with a minimum charge of £30 plus account charges of £2.50 per stock per half year. Now, this may be OK if you only want to buy a single stock, but what happens when you get addicted to the Fool US and decide to set up a Beating the Dow portfolio, or you want to buy AOL, and then Coke, and Microsoft and . . . and . . .? You will end up paying simply tooooooo much in commissions.

No, DON'T DO IT FOOLS! *Consider instead opening up a brokerage account with a US Internet broker. It really is easy, and you will save yourself lots of money. On the Fool US site you can review the various Internet brokers' charges (and dream of the day that we get such low costs for buying and selling shares in the*

UK) at the Discount Brokerage Center.

We can't say this enough: opening a brokerage account with a US discount broker really is simple. You just print off the application forms online, fill them out, sign them and post them by snail mail (they need a real signature) with a US cheque (or 'check', if you are American), or else wire them the funds from a UK bank account, which takes a few days. (Some brokers actually require to send you the forms first via snail mail to make sure you are who you say you are and are living where you say you are.) Within a few days of sending off the forms and wiring the money you will get confirmation that your account is open and you are up and running and able to trade directly in US stocks from the comfort of your own computer, surrounded as it is by half-eaten tuna sandwiches, mouldy cups of coffee and three-week-old copies of the Financial Times. *Oh yes, we can see you!*

Of course, it's not all such plain sailing. You do have to put up with the disgrace of being termed a 'Non-resident alien' by the American tax authorities. You see, there are certain formalities concerning the tax treatment of your US shares, and these formalities must be clarified with the brokerage house when the account is opened. Most individuals who are not US citizens must complete a W-8 form (downloadable from the web site of the US Internal Revenue Service), which is a certificate of foreign status, and return it to the broker.

The specific rules governing how these accounts are taxed are described in IRS Publication 515 (Withholding of tax on non-resident aliens) and IRS Publication 901 (Tax treaties). The tax treaty issue is especially important. You can view these publications online at the IRS web site, www.irs.ustreas.gov/prod/forms_pubs/formpub.html. *If the individual's country of residence has an agreement (tax treaty) with the US government, then those rules apply and certain forms of income may have tax withheld on them at source, notably dividend income.*

If your country of residence has no agreement with the US, then you should complete the 1001 form (exemption form), also usually available to print off at the online broker's web site, and no tax will then be withheld.

Of course, US citizens living abroad are not required to fill out either of these forms, since they are in any case required to report their worldwide income to the US annually and are automatically subject to US taxation laws. If you are an American citizen, no matter where you live, you cannot escape the LOOOOONG *arm of the US Internal Revenue Service.*

Worried about reliability? Worried that you may be risking your money with some fly-by-night company? Firstly, the financial regulations concerning public companies in the US are stricter than any in the UK – including four-times-a-year company reporting. In the US, every financial report from every listed company is *available on the Net, in its entirety, for everyone to see. Now, that we like. Secondly, any broker you choose should be indemnified up to at least $500,000 by the Securities Investor Protection Corporation (SIPC). Many carry far higher indemnity provisions than this.*

What about currency fluctuations over the years? Currently, the pound is very strong, meaning it will buy a lot of US dollars. What if it gets even stronger in 30 years' time when you want to bring your dollars back to spend in the UK? It might happen that way, yes, or alternatively the pound may be weaker then than it is now. In our opinion, there is risk inherent in any enterprise, but there's idiotic risk and there's Foolish risk. At the kinds of returns that great American companies have provided over decades (like Coca-Cola's 17 per cent on average every year since 1918) and with the general strength of both our economies, this is a Foolish risk and not one which we think will figure hugely in your financial equations a few decades from now.

Can you afford not to invest in the US? Post your thoughts and experiences on transatlantic investing to our 'All US Shares' message board. And don't forget the not inconsiderable resource of the US site's message boards – all 2500 of them.

Fool on!

So, there you have it, straight from the mouths of Fools. The Internet is shrinking the world of investment. Buy quality US companies, but don't get seduced into day trading US stocks, spending all your waking hours glued to the computer screen, worrying about a half-percentage point change here or there. Life is too short for that. Far too short.

And how do you decide which US stocks to invest in? Well, that is a subject for a book in itself, but just to see the amount of information available free of charge to any investor in US companies, just check out the US Securities and Exchange Commission's company filings database, EDGAR, at www.sec.gov/edaux/searches.htm, where US companies are obliged to file their quarterly reports, for all to see. The Motley Fool US web site at www.fool.com is a must and the NASDAQ site at www.nasdaq.com, is also to be recommended. The markets over there are much more geared up to the private investor, and the Internet brings all that information into your home. If you're going abroad for your investments, the US should be your first stop.

What about other countries?

Unfortunately, the wealth of data available in the US, and the openness of its presentation, is far ahead of any other country in the world. So far.

Whatever you think about the euro, it's clear that within the next few years it will be possible to trade on any market in Europe from the comfort of your lounge, office, bedroom, study, bathroom(?), outhouse(?!), or wherever your personal computer is located. Not too far behind that may be the ability to trade in world markets at any time of the day, as increasingly they will open for longer hours each day. Worried everyone will turn into investing junkies, using their evenings to trade shares in Holland, South Africa and Japan simultaneously, whilst shorting stocks in the US and closing positions in London before climbing the stairs with their mug of Ovaltine . . . ?

Well, that's not too likely to happen, but global 24-hour trading is likely not far away. There is a fair amount of ground to be covered first, though, and a few barriers to break through. First of all, the language. Any UK investor would be at something of a disadvantage if they could not understand any of the literature or on-screen research about the company concerned.

And then there is the currency risk. The pound and the US dollar are pretty strong, stable currencies, but the same cannot be said for many other currencies beyond the euro. Look at the horrendous instability of a currency like the Russian rouble, for instance, which could be enough to wipe out many private investors who dabbled in that high risk market. It's *mafiosi* who make money there, not investors.

Critically, too, the quality of financial disclosure and the degree of openness and honesty we are used to in the UK and the US are lacking in many international markets, especially in the developing world, and in Asia. Insider trading, corruption and share price manipulation can be rife, and it is impossible to get reliable information about companies and their prospects. Investing in these sorts of nations just isn't worth it from an individual's point of view, being more speculation and gambling than investing.

If a club really did want to invest in the developing world, or in a nation with more dubious markets, then there are many unit or investment trusts that invest in foreign markets. Here, we would break our Foolish principle of not investing in managed unit trusts because of their persistent underperformance and high charges, and suggest that if your club does have a burning desire to get into these kinds of investments, maybe this is the way to go. All the literature is in English, and the investments are spread across a wide range of companies in any particular market or geographical area. The problems of financial instability, corruption, political uncertainty and poor reporting remain, however. Fund managers genuinely have a harder job in such markets, and you will have to pay for it, so that will eat into your returns.

Frankly, it's probably better for investment clubs to stick with the UK, the US and perhaps Europe for the time being.

And one final note: watch out for the Motley Fool extending the Foolish word to other European web sites through 1999 and 2000. Initially, these will be in the language of the countries concerned, but it is later planned to translate key content into English, providing an introduction to the markets of those countries.

11

How can I learn more?

In a time of drastic change it is the learners who inherit the future. The learned usually find themselves equipped to live in a world that no longer exists.
Eric Hoffer

Knowledge is a wonderful thing, and *Homo sapiens*, as a species, is equipped with a brain capable of absorbing an awful lot of it. Unfortunately, you do need to have a little spare time on your hands in order to learn most things, and the stock market is no exception. The good news is that, while the City professionals are trying to bamboozle you with unfamiliar jargon, there are many publications that use easy-to-understand language and which are quite 'user friendly' for the novice.

Most of your financial knowledge will come from reading, of course. You may have never even looked at the City pages in your daily newspaper, but six months from now you could find yourself scanning the share prices on Teletext and reading press comments about a company with great interest. If you subscribe to satellite or cable TV, there are a number of TV channels which provide continuous financial programming.

Before we go any further, though, just one or two thoughts on the nature of financial journalism in general. There are some excellent financial journalists who provide informed comment on business events. Unfortunately, there is also a short-term focus in the media – which has to sell papers or catch viewers – and this can make it quite misleading for those interested in the long-term approach to investing. Headlines like '50 billion pounds wiped off the price of shares today' often follow a transient drop in the market following a prolonged period of gains, of far more than a mere 50 billion pounds. Such headlines are needlessly alarmist and designed to capitalize on the public's fear of another crash, like the one we had in 1929 and haven't had since. This emphasis on the short-term movement of the market and share prices of individual companies instead of the long term – where we should all be looking as individual investors or clubs – is worth watching out for and making a mental note of as you see it. Above all, don't let the media spook you! If they're saying it's a catastrophe, a disaster, a horror, a meltdown, please be assured that it probably isn't. And if you're after a somewhat different viewpoint, you can always check into the Motley Fool online, where you'll find the Fools singularly unimpressed by news of calamities, shocks, collapses and what-have-you.

So, while there is plenty of information out there,

use it well and maintain a healthy sense of scepticism.

The Bullworker Technique

Most people will remember advertisements in comics and magazines for a chest expander called the 'Bullworker'. This was a vicious-looking contraption developed by a prize-winning bodybuilder who claimed that using Bullworker for fifteen minutes a day would turn you from 'Mr Puny-verse' into 'Mr Universe' in just a few weeks.

Well, fifteen minutes' reading a day will not turn you into the world's most successful investor, but it will enable you to get a grasp on what is happening in the world financial markets, as well as helping you make rational and informed investment decisions based on your own findings. If you spend just a few minutes a day keeping abreast of what's happening in the world of investing, you will see your financial savvy grow to levels you would never have thought possible.

Where to start?

Online, of course! And start with the Motley Fool (please). You'll find a variety of daily articles keeping you abreast of the financial news. Naturally, all with a Foolish spin.

Newspapers are also a good way to keep up with what's happening. The *Financial Times* is an excellent source of news and a readable newspaper. The Saturday edition contains a weekend 'Money' section packed with good articles, useful information – things like which companies are due to report their results in the coming week, and the reports of directors dealing in their own company's shares. *Sunday Business* is a weekly pink broadsheet newspaper with an easy-to-read style. You will often find information in this paper that you will not read anywhere else. If you are a novice, then you may find the financial jargon used in the *FT*, *Sunday Business* and the broadsheets like *The Times* or the *Telegraph* a bit beyond you to begin with, but do persevere. Of course, you could always set your sights a bit lower.

Most of the other newspapers have financial pages of varying quality. Use your judgement, because that's what you should be developing.

Magazines and Periodicals

One of the most popular periodicals is, without a doubt, *Investors Chronicle.* Many people are genuinely frightened of this publication when they first start out, and convince themselves that it is for professionals only. However, after you have read a couple of issues, you might be amazed to find that you can actually understand most of the stuff printed inside the covers. It's worth a read, but don't get lured into following their 'share tips'. As with any other source of investing information – including the Fool – use your discretion and make your own decisions. Don't blindly follow those of others.

As for monthly magazines, the best on offer would seem to be *Bloomberg Money*.

Tipsheets

As soon as your name and address gets linked with anything financial, then you end up on a mailing list and you start to receive letters offering you riches beyond your wildest dreams. Financial tipsheets are plentiful in number and dubious in quality. Yes, some are better than others (and one or two are even actually pretty good, but they are swamped by the bad ones). There are even some that masquerade as tipsheets, but are actually just advertisements for the companies they promote.

There tends to be a lot more activity in the marketing of tipsheets during boom periods for the stock market. Unfortunately, this may not be the most advantageous time to buy. What often happens is that a tipsheet will feature a company and recommend it as a Strong Buy, and the Market Makers – the people who set the prices of shares – will consequently mark the price of that stock higher as a result, at the opening of that morning's trade. (This also happens with the *Investors Chronicle* share tips, except often *before* the edition is published. Any ideas how that might happen?) Investors receiving the tipsheet also decide to buy the stock, and the demand sends the price ever higher. After a couple of weeks, the buying momentum stops, perhaps some investors take some profits, and the price drops down again, sometimes to a lower point than it was when tipped. Often the share which has been tipped is a penny share, which requires very little activity to move its share price – another reason not to invest in them.

At the Fool we recommend that all investors do their own research, and with an investment club, there are potentially 20 members who can share in that research. So make the most of people's opinions and encourage them to speak at meetings! Do your own research, and stand by your decisions. Do not assume everyone (anyone) else is an expert.

By all means, if you wish to do so as a club, take a subscription to a reputable newsletter – *The Analyst* is a popular and well respected publication – as a source of information and research. But do not rely solely on its recommendations to make your investment decisions. Try to substantiate them via other sources, perhaps even the company itself. Better still, save the money you would have spent on a subscription, and do your own research.

Some tipsheets use shameful advertising to try to sell themselves. They claim that individual investors simply can't invest successfully themselves, that the author has insider access to City rumours, has 'eyes and ears in every wine bar in the City', and other such nonsense. Another UK Fool, Alan Oscroft, received a 'special, limited time only' invitation to subscribe to one of these publications recently, and penned the following parody of it for that day's Daily Fool on the Web.

Hey, Fools, wanna know how a £1000 gamble on the horses could have turned into £1.4 million? Why you couldn't choose a better time to start gambling on the turf? What are the five most exciting fillies on the racing calendar right now?

If you want to know more, what you need is 'Alan Oscroft's Red Hot Racing Tips'. If you subscribe now, through this exclusive, invitation-only opportunity, never to be repeated (unless I don't get enough money this time round), you'll get those first five hot tips absolutely free! If you've ever dreamed of making a packet on the gee-gees, then I'm writing to you today to invite you to accept my 'insider' tips on the best nags around – tips that are whispered wherever professional gamblers gather at Epsom, Newmarket, Ripon, Cheltenham. This isn't a simple investment opportunity, of course. No, it's much more than that. It's a chance for excitement, a chance to be a confidential insider in the world of racing. Think of the adrenalin that will flow every time you get a tip that is exclusive to you (and all the other people who pay me). Think of that first 10-grand cheque from your bookie!

The world of racing is a world full of nobby insiders, who sit there all day in their silly hats, with their binoculars slung around their necks, passing insider tips to each other like there's no tomorrow. . . 'Psst, Tarquin, it's Mother's Ruin, a grand on the nose will set you up . . . Bishop's Withers has got a dodgy fetlock, the smart money's on Christ's Chin . . . Spazpecker Windsock in the 3:30 is nobbled, don't put a penny on him.' Yes, I know it makes you angry to learn that these nobs are getting it handed to them on a plate, but now you can be a privileged part of it, too!

Suppose you had a spare £1000. If you'd followed the insider tips that I, through my many and varied contacts in the racing world, could have offered to you, you could have made your million and then some! Firstly, if you'd put the grand on Moutahddee in the 2.05 at Newmarket on Friday, you'd have turned it into £5000 in the blink of an eye. Next, following my hot tips, over to the 3.20 at Ripon, where you would have put your five grand on Prairie Wolf at 6-1, netting £35,000. Back, then, to Newmarket, just in time for Munjiz, in the 3.45 at odds of 9-1, bringing a total so far of £350,000. After that, you would only have needed to double your money twice more to net £1.4 million. And, I'm sure you'd agree, after results as good as those I've just shown you, just doubling your money should be child's play.

OK, Fools, back to Planet Earth. My apologies for my flight of fancy, but I have just received an exclusive, launch-year priority invitation to subscribe to a penny share tipsheet, and I got quite carried away there in my little world of fantasy. The invitation tells me how I could have turned £1000 into £1.2 million, using nothing more than the miracle of hindsight – a rare gift, indeed. I'm sure none of the rest of us could have gone back through history and spotted the companies that have already made it big, right? It is offering me a totally free introductory subscription, and all I need to do is give them all my bank details so they can take what they want by direct debit. All I then need to do is cancel after the first edition and owe nothing! Does this sound familiar these days?

And what of the five free tips on offer? Well, I don't get those until after I've sent back the direct debit stuff, of course, but I do get some tantalizing glimpses. Try this one . . . 'Every couple of minutes, another person in Britain dies from a stroke or heart disease . . . In September, a tiny British company gained regulatory approval to market . . . a test for detecting susceptibility to heart disease.' September? Hot news? This Fool is not impressed. We can't be sure who this tip is, of course, but I suspect a look over on the Motley Fool's Shield Diagnostics message board might give us a clue – and a wealth of opinions helping us to do our own rational fundamental analysis, of course, instead of blindly swallowing what the tipsheets tell us. And as for the fresh hot tip, direct from contacts in the City? About as fresh as the lump of Stilton in my fridge, more like it!

So don't forget, if you follow the Fool, you'll put no faith in gurus or get-rich-quick schemes, and you will not subscribe to tipsheets that promise untold wealth. No, you'll learn, step by step, how easy it is to make your own decisions, and you'll settle for the good reliable solid growth over many years that comes from sensible investments in good companies. Most of all, you will learn that the only real decision-maker that you can trust is yourself, because you are the only one who really has your interests at heart.

Books

'But if I shouldn't subscribe to tipsheets, where do I get all this information?' we hear you cry. Well, you really do need to learn what to look for in a company, after all. As a novice, you need to find out the techniques used by the world's greatest investors. We can all invest with hindsight; what we really need to do is to identify the great companies *before* they become great companies.

You need to read some books. And buying them within a club spreads the cost too. A £20 book costs each member a measly pound if you have 20 members.

On the Fool web site you can gain access to the Fools bookshop. Just select the book(s) you require, type in your credit/debit card where indicated, then wait about four days. The books turn up by post.

Simple, isn't it? Alternatively, just go into your local bookshop and order them.

Here are brief details of some of the books on offer:
The Motley Fool UK Investment Workbook by David Berger and Bruce Jackson

A 1999 addition to the UK stable of books (along with this one). Work through your own finances and learn how to read company accounts, painlessly. Really.

The Motley Fool UK Investment Guide by David Berger, David Gardner and Tom Gardner
You've heard enough about it already. Go buy it (pretty please).

The Motley Fool's Rule Breakers and Rule Makers by David and Tom Gardner
This US Motley Fool book is a stockpicking guide that teaches you how to find really great companies, the ones that break the old rules, and make the new rules. It is a handbook for business, really, rather than just an investment book.

The Warren Buffett Portfolio by Robert Hagstrom
The latest of Robert Hagstrom's books about the Buffett and, as with the others, very readable. If you read this book and you're hungering for the actual words of the great man himself, then you'll find his annual 'Letter to shareholders' for the past fifteen years at his web site: www.berkshirehathaway.com

Beating the Street by Peter Lynch
As fund manager of Fidelity's superbly performing Magellan fund in the 1980s, Peter Lynch attained guru status in the US. In this book he gives good

insight into his stockpicking methods and writes clearly and well.

Common Stocks and Uncommon Profits by Philip Fisher
This is an investment classic, and a wonderful guide to understanding a company's core business and the importance of becoming familiar with the people that run it. Fisher provides a number of ways to better understand what these companies do, and why, who they are, and whether you should continue to invest in them.

The Intelligent Investor by Ben Graham
A simple analytical framework for investors as well as a definition of what investing really means, which is to say 'investing' shouldn't be confused with 'trading'. Very hard going at times, but an investment classic.

What Works on Wall Street by James O'Shaughnessy
Mechanical investment strategies and a good section on the psychology of being an investor. This is the work that laid the foundation built upon by the Fool's *Beating the Dow* and *Beating the Footsie* mechanical strategies. Recently revised and well worth reading.

Accounting for Growth by Terry Smith
Terry Smith throws some interesting light on the devious ways in which companies spruce up their balance sheets.

Read on and learn, you Fool, and the financial world can be yours!

12

Are we restricted to buying shares?

There is no finer investment for any community than putting milk into babies.
Sir Winston Churchill

Most investment discussion at the Motley Fool relates to stocks and shares, proven to be the most consistent, reliable and effective means to grow your money over time. Sooner or later in an investment club meeting, however, someone is going to come up with a wild card suggestion for the club's next investment. 'Why do we only ever invest in shares?' they will say. 'What about-?'. It is possible that an occasional suggestion might make sense, but the odds are heavily stacked against it. Most 'alternative' ideas are just wacky nonsense, and you need to be prepared to deal with them.

Let's take a look at what they may suggest, along with any problems and pitfalls you may encounter.

Freehold property – to receive a rental income

Although the prospect of purchasing a property may seem laughable to you now, even if your club has only moderate investment success, in a few years' time you might easily have enough cash to buy a small flat or bedsit in the North of England and possibly even in the home counties or the South.

'Why would we want to do that?' you ask. Well, let us assume that you spent £30,000 on a one-bedroom flat and arranged a tenancy at £300 per month. On the face of it, that looks like a tempting 12 per cent annual yield, *plus* any capital appreciation in the value of the property. No risk either, and no short-term volatility. That's got to be good, hasn't it? Plenty of banks and Wise financial institutions are heavily selling mortgages to let these days, and that alone should be enough to raise the odd alarm bell or two, don't you think? So think again then, and think carefully. There are many things that will conspire to bring that headline 12 per cent down . . .

a) *Income Tax.* All rental money received is subject to income tax at your marginal rate, with no allowances at all. It is all taxable. You have no £7000 per member in personal Capital Gains Tax allowance. You have to report it all in your tax returns too, and that adds to the workload of one member, probably your long-suffering treasurer.

b) *Bad tenants.* Most people who have let a property

have at least one horror story relating to the tenants, either through non-payment of rent or by causing physical damage to the property. So that's lost income, and it takes off some of that 12 per cent headline rate, doesn't it? Does it still sound risk-free?

c) *No tenants.* So you are going to get 100 per cent occupancy, are you? Oh no, you're not! You will find times when the property is difficult to let and you get no rental income at all. You've still got to pay the council tax though, and keep the gas, water and electricity ticking over. Can you see that 12 per cent slipping further away?

d) *Agent's fees.* Are you going to manage the property yourselves? Find tenants, draw up contracts, handle the maintenance, clean the place up between tenants? That's a lot of work, and you will really need to place it in the hands of a managing agent. That'll take about 15 per cent off your gross rents for starters. With all these expenses, you'll be lucky to be left with 4 or 5 per cent in real returns.

e) *Property devaluation.* Oh yes, there's no guarantee of capital appreciation. Prices fall sometimes too, particularly in those nice cheap areas of the country where you thought you might get a bargain. Not everywhere appreciates at London rates.

f) *A member leaves the club.* How do you value his

share? Do you arrange a current valuation? Who pays for this? How does the club realize the cash in order to redeem the departing member's holding? In short, loads of problems.

Freehold property – for use as a holiday home

Come on, what is this, an investment club or a timesharing agency? If your members want to pool their resources to buy a holiday home to share, then that's up to them. But it's nothing to do with investment, is it? So let them do it outside of the club. In the club, you have to remain focused on your goals, and that reinforces the need for a good constitution (for the club, that is – we're not talking about your alcohol capacity and your ability to stay up late), and a clear set of rules.

The Fine Wines Market

Every now and then you'll hear about the possibilities of investing in fine wines. It often starts with a cold call from a smooth talker trying to convince you to invest in the vintage stuff. The minimum investment is usually something like half a case of Chateau Mouton Rothschild 1996, or similar, coming in at around £1500 or so. They'll tell you how well good Bordeaux has appreciated over the last seven or eight years, comparing the original purchase price per bottle with the current retail price. Hey, remember that old Foolish principle – don't buy what you don't understand. Know about great wines, do you? Well, if you did, you'd know that they need to be stored in good cellars for many years, and that the eventual buyers will need some proof of where they have been kept. You can't just keep them under the stairs and hope buyers will trust you to have stored them well. Nope, you have to pay for professional cellarage, and that is expensive and only becomes cost-effective when you have hundreds, or even thousands, of cases. You have to pay commission to that sweet-talker who is selling the stuff too, both when you buy and when you finally sell, perhaps 5 per cent each time. Ouch!

Another thing you will realize, if you know about wine, is that we have had an exceptionally good decade for Bordeaux prices (and when we are thinking of wines for investment, there is really nowhere else to look). Three great years in 1988, 1989 and 1990, and then a procession of dismal harvests. This coincided with increasing demand from the new wealthy of the Far East, particularly Japan, who just didn't care what they paid, provided they got a good label. The last three or four years have seen quality harvests, and the Asian yuppies who previously clamoured for the stuff are now nursing their overdrafts instead. Are we going to see another Bordeaux price bubble? What do you think?

So go buy a bottle from time to time, and enjoy drinking it. Something for your investment club, though? Hmmm, we don't think so.

Horses

Another frequently suggested 'alternative' investment is the part ownership of a racehorse. But have you ever really worked out why racehorse owners are so wealthy? They didn't make their money from racing. No, they made it elsewhere and now they are spending it! Horse racing costs a packet to take part in. Leave this one for Ealing comedies and Brian Rix farces.

Premium Bonds

Does this one sound like a more reasonable alternative investment for a club? Big blocks of £10,000 Premium Bonds tend to win pretty regular prizes, and of course the initial investment is always protected. But look rationally at the returns you can reasonably expect. Do they come close to the 12 per cent per year that the stock market has averaged since 1918? No, they don't come close. There is the possibility of winning big prizes, but that's just gambling, and if that's what you want, buy a lottery ticket.

The National Lottery

You cannot be serious! This is gambling, not investing, and requires no skill or logical analysis at all. If you want to gamble on the lottery, and you want to increase your chances by sharing with other people, then join a lottery syndicate. Leave investment clubs for investors.

Multi-Level Marketing

Multi-Level Marketing, otherwise known as Pyramid Selling, is a business proposition that promises much and delivers little. The products are often very good, and it can work for some people, for those who start it early. Such schemes work best of all for the founders. But those people are not you or I, and it really has nothing to do with an investment club. If individuals are mad enough to want to try it, individual members should do it for themselves. Remember those all-important club rules.

So why mention it here? For two reasons:

1) Someone once sent H+G a load of stuff on an MLM product and asked us to 'invest' in the business. We didn't.
2) I have a great (and perfectly true) story which I always said I would put in a book if I ever wrote one. I may not write another one, and this is my chance to squeeze the story in. I make no apologies. It has nothing to do with investment clubs, but hey, everyone needs a break some time, so read on and relax.

Some years ago I was out of work and turned to Multi-Level Marketing on various people's recommendations. If you ever decide to get involved with anything like this (and I guess most of us have either been approached, or at least know someone who has given it a go), one of the first things you notice when you turn up at the introductory meetings is the mixture of cars in the car park. This is because the people at the top of the pyramid (the up-line) are making some serious money and there may well be a few Mercs or Beemers hanging around. Parked alongside, and in far greater quantity, are the cars of the hopefuls, the would-be MLM-ers, people who maybe are out of work and going along to see what it's all about. They have X-reg Volvos, C-reg Escorts, or maybe old Toyotas.

In any event, I attended a meeting for an MLM company called Benchmark (they no longer exist, by the way) and they had two products. One was a personal fire extinguisher called 'Fireosol', and the other was a barrier/moisturising cream called 'Dermashield'. Both products were pretty good, I have to say.

Now, the Fireosol demonstration was very impressive. There we were in this hotel conference room, about 50 of us, and a person was telling us about personal fire extinguishers, when all of a sudden, he doused the flip chart display with lighter fuel and set fire to it. He didn't break off his sentence, just carried on talking as though nothing was happening, whilst this mini-inferno was raging away at the front of the room. As smoke began to form and gently billow up to the ceiling, he reached for the Fireosol, sprayed once, *Pcchhht*... the fire was out. Very, very impressive. The people broke into spontaneous applause (once they had stopped coughing), and clamoured for more information about this incredible product.

Now I was thinking ahead here . . . A good friend of mine was a market trader on Canvey Island in Essex, and they had a very busy Sunday market. If he could get me a casual pitch there one week, and I could get a case or two of these things, I could set up a flip chart, set light to it, wait for a crowd to gather, then extinguish the flames! I'd be beating them off with sticks! I'd probably sell out within an hour or two! Wow, things were looking up!

I had a word with my friend, and he in turn spoke to the market manager who said that if I turned up early one Sunday, he would see what he could do, bearing in mind I would hardly need any space.

I spoke to my up-line, who, upon discovering that I wanted to order a couple of cases of these things, thought it was a fantastic idea. The products arrived by courier the following day, and my bank account was about £300 lighter. Still, never mind, there'll be that and more going in next week, I thought.

The next thing was to purchase my 'props'. I went to a mid-week boot sale and purchased an old flip chart and adjustable easel for a tenner, and then went to the newsagent to buy some long matches and some lighter fuel. I was set.

The following Sunday at 5.30 a.m. I loaded up my car and set off for the market. It was a warm August morning with a fair bit of high cloud in the sky. I saw the market manager, who directed me to a pitch slap-bang at the end of the main aisle. Perfect! I could see all the way down to the entrance. 'The crowds will be running up here later,' I thought. I could hardly wait for the market to open.

It seemed an eternity before the first few people drifted in. It got busy at about 11 o'clock, my friend had told me, so I didn't really expect much before then. But at about 9:20, there were about 30 people wandering towards me, so I thought now was the time to strike! I doused my flip chart in lighter fluid, and reached for the matches. After two or three attempts, I got a match to actually light, held it against the flip chart and . . . nothing. No burst of flame, nothing. The match was now burning my fingers, so I dropped that and tried again. I looked round anxiously, to see even more people in the aisle and heading my way. Great, maybe a blessing in disguise, more people will see it now, after all I'd practised all my patter and got it off pat – come on, lighter fuel, come on, matches – still nothing. I could not get this stuff to light. Now the smokers amongst you may have sussed out what was happening. In any event, it was a neighbouring trader, who had been watching with some amusement, who then told me that it was the lighter fuel *vapour* that ignites, not the liquid. Of course, being in the open air, it was evaporating before the flame got anywhere near it! All I'd got left was a soggy flip chart!

Right, I thought, I'm not beaten, so I lit the match

first, and then simultaneously poured the fluid over the chart. WOOF! At last, a ball of flame shot into the air, and we were in business. I turned around . . . and the aisle was empty. Everyone had gone past or had disappeared into the other offshoot aisles. 'Oi,' said my neighbouring trader, as the flames started licking against the side of the canvas awning at the side of his table, 'put those flames out.' I had to oblige, of course, and no-one saw it except for me, him and a few other distinctly unimpressed people. Never mind, not to be beaten, I moved the easel a few more feet away from his pitch, and prepared to try again. It had been a bad start, but I'd got the hang of it now, and come 11 o'clock when it was packed, it wouldn't be a problem. Things could not get any worse.

And then it started to rain.

Well, not rain exactly, it was that very fine misty drizzle that was not enough to actually stop you doing anything. However, the cumulative effect of standing out in it for about 20 minutes meant that not only was I pretty wet but so was my flip chart and I don't think I could have set light to it with a flame thrower. Never mind, I had a contingency plan. I had also ordered 200 promotional leaflets and had stuck address labels on all of these. I would just give them to interested parties and make the sales later. After all, only 5 per cent of the population actually have any firefighting equipment at all, so I should be OK to shift a few . . .

Now, for those who don't know, Canvey Island is

home to a massive methane gas terminal, and it has been long rumoured that one day it will blow. If it does, most of the island will go with it. Consequently, almost *every* person on Canvey has at least one fire extinguisher at home. I reckon the local council must have given them out free with voting cards. This was rapidly turning into a very bad day now. There I was, broke, soaking wet, trying to perform dramatic firefighting demonstrations using a soggy flip chart and attempting to sell fire extinguishers to people who already had them. In the rain. I think it was about 1.00 when another trader came over to me and said 'Why don't you go home?' I took his advice.

I continued to try and make a go of Multi-Level Marketing until I telephoned one of my best and oldest friends to invite her and her husband to dinner. 'Hello, Mark, what are you selling this time?' she said. That shook me rigid. I had no idea that I had come across as nothing but a salesman to the people closest to me, and I did not want to give that impression at all. I gave it up the following day, and have not considered it since.

And neither should you.

13

Right, I'm convinced. What do I do now?

The present is the ever moving shadow that divides yesterday from tomorrow. In that lies hope.
Frank Lloyd Wright

Well, you know what they say: 'Strike while the iron is hot'. Congratulations if you have read this far, for you are on the way to becoming a Fool. If you are flicking through the book, and have stopped at this point, go back and read it from the beginning. It's not a big book, it won't take long.

Whatever you decide to do, whether it's to start a club or join a club, it is going to take you a few weeks to get things going. But you can start now. Put the kettle on, make yourself a cup of something, find a quiet spot, and start reading the financial pages of whatever daily paper comes to hand. And if you don't have a paper, pop out and buy one. Then follow these simple steps.

Setting up a new club

a) First of all, order the ProShare Manual from ProShare (020 7600 0984).
b) In the few days before it arrives try to get hold of at least one of the books in the recommended reading list in Chapter 11.
c) Keep reading the financial pages of your newspaper. Don't worry if it means nothing at this stage; you are familiarizing yourself with the layout and the jargon.
d) Just for fun, pick three or four shares out of the paper whose names you recognize or products you like and follow the share prices each day, along with keeping up on any news about them. This is called a 'paper portfolio' and is a confidence-building exercise.
e) Make contact with a few friends and tell them what you are planning to do. See if you can get at least ten people interested. You may be surprised at the response you get!
f) Try and arrange an informal get together when you can all go through the rules and constitution.
g) See if anybody is willing to be a club official. There should be at least a chairman, secretary and treasurer. If you are starting the club, be prepared to be an official yourself. Make sure that willing parties know exactly what they are taking on!
h) Subject to everyone being happy about the rules

and having members prepared to be club officials, it is now time to call the inaugural meeting.

i) Find a suitable venue. This could be in a pub, a restaurant, a pub, a church hall, someone's home or a pub. Sorry, did I mention pub more than once? Oh well, if you *do* meet in a pub, make it a night when it is less likely to be busy. A side room would be ideal.

j) Arrange for a set of rules and a constitution to be copied from the ProShare manual for each attending member. It would help if someone has access to a photocopier. If not, perhaps all the members can chip in with the cost.

k) Fix an agenda for the meeting, and make a copy for each member. A typical inaugural meeting agenda can be found in the ProShare manual, but these should include the election of the club officials, the adoption of the rules and constitution, and the appointment of club bankers and stockbrokers.

l) Have the meeting! You may wish to discuss investment strategy, or you may wish to leave such discussions until it is time to make the first purchases. Talk about monthly subscriptions. Set a level that everyone is comfortable with and that they are prepared to lose. Remember, the prime function is educational.

m) If all goes well, set a date for the next meeting.

n) Make sure the secretary sends the minutes of the meeting out to each member *prior* to the next meeting.
o) Learn, laugh and make money.

Joining a club

a) You may have been approached by a friend to join a new or an existing investment club. Great! Having read this book you will be able to be an active member.
b) If you are looking to approach existing clubs, this can be tricky as many clubs only open their ranks to people who are known to them. However, ProShare have a feature in their quarterly magazine in which clubs advertise for members by postcode. Alternatively, head over to the Motley Fool's Investment Clubs message board and post a message asking if there are any vacancies in clubs in your area.

Taking more control over your financial future

It may well be that the idea of an investment club appeals but for one reason or another you are unable to do anything about it at the moment. Not to worry, you can still take steps to protect and enhance your future by learning to invest the Foolish way. Plough through some of those books in Chapter 11, visit the Fool's web site at www.fool.co.uk and off you go! And if you think that your family and friends can also benefit from your new found knowledge, then any Motley Fool book makes a great stocking filler at Christmas (especially this one!).

14

And finally, Cyril . . .

However big the Fool, there is always a bigger Fool to admire him.
Nicolas Boileau-Despréaux

It was Esther Rantzen who turned the above into a catchphrase at the end of her *That's Life* programme. Cyril Fletcher was the recipient, and he would respond with the words 'and finally, Esther' before concluding the show, sometimes with one of his 'odd odes'.

Well done and thank you for reading this book. I will assume that you have enjoyed it, otherwise you would not have got this far. If you purchased it yourself, you have made a good investment. If it was a present, then the person who gave it to you obviously has fantastic taste and they clearly have your best interests at heart. If you have stolen it, then you have probably hit upon the only occasion when crime does actually pay. You should feel so enriched by the experience that you should go back to where you lifted it from and purchase two copies to send to friends.

I have relayed my experiences in setting up and running investment clubs for both your education and amusement. This book has been aimed at people with little or no experience of stock market investment and consequently the traditional highbrow language has been abandoned in favour of (I hope) easily readable text and examples to illustrate how straightforward the world of finance can be. This book will affect your life, maybe in a tiny way, maybe not now, but at some point I am sure that you will remember something you have read within these pages and it will make you stop and think about whatever it was you were going to do. The book may have reached its end, but this could mark the beginning of a new hobby for *you*, the beginning of a period where you take control of your financial future, the beginning of something that could touch your life in the same way that it has touched mine.

H&G Investments has received more attention (to date) than any other investment club in the country. At the time the club made its debut media appearance on *Channel 4 News* in January 1997 there were 300 or so clubs in the country. This number had increased ten-fold by January 1999.

Personally, I would love to think that there will be another ten-fold increase in the next two years as a direct result of this publication, although another increase like that is highly unlikely. But if only a few of you set up or join investment clubs purely because you have read this book, then it will have achieved its purpose. If I have also convinced you to don a coat of motley, sport a belled cap and join the ranks of the Fools, crusading for common sense in investment and fairness for all, then so much the better.

Fool on!

The Fool's Guide through the Jargon Jungle

Advisory stockbroker Stockbrokers who offer advice on which shares to buy and sell. We don't favour using them. See **execution-only stockbroker** and **churn.**
Alternative Investment Market (AIM) AIM opened in 1995 for small, growing companies. It's less difficult to be listed here than on the London **Stock Exchange** and shares are higher risk and more likely to be difficult to buy and sell. See **liquidity.**
Analyst A financial professional who analyses securities to determine a 'fair' or 'intrinsic' value for those securities. The term is generally applied to almost any professional investor who does research of some kind.
Annualize Taking an item measured over a certain period and restating it on an annual basis. For instance, if it costs £10 million every month to run a factory, the annualized cost is £10 million × 12, or £120 million, since there are 12 months in a year.
Annual report A yearly statement of a public company's operating and financial performance

punctuated by pictures of families enjoying the firm's products and/or services.

Annuity The investment you purchase with your pension fund which will provide you with a regular income in your retirement. They are intrinsically poor investments.

Appreciation Increase in the price (or value) of a share or other asset. Appreciation is one component of total return.

Balance sheet An important financial report regularly issued by companies. It provides a look at a company's assets, debts and shareholder equity at one particular point in time.

Bank of England Set up in 1649, the 'Old Lady of Threadneedle Street' has responsibility for regulating the banking industry and since 1997 sets interest rates to help the government meet its inflation targets. The stock market hangs on the Bank's interest rate pronouncements.

Bankruptcy: When a company owes more than it can pay, or when its debts exceed its assets, it's bankrupt.

Bear So you think that the market is headed south? You're bracing yourself for a crash or correction? You feel that share XYZ will soon be taking a tumble? Guess what – you're a bear! Bears are investors with pessimistic outlooks, as opposed to **bulls.**

Beating the Footsie A mechanical investment strategy, based on buying large cap shares with a high **dividend yield** on a regular, rotational basis.

Bid-offer spread The difference between the bid price (at which the holder can sell shares) and the offer price (at which the holder can buy shares). On occasion this can be quite large and depends on the equity's underlying price, **liquidity**, volatility and a number of other factors. Many **unit trusts** also have a bid-offer spread and effectively this amounts to an *extra* **exit charge** when the investor sells.

Big Bang The first big shake-up of the stock market in October 1986, when computers were introduced into the trading process for the first time. This was followed in 1996 by the introduction of **CREST** and then in 1997 by **Big Bang II**.

Big Bang II 20 October 1997. The use of a computer-driven trading system to cut out the middlemen in share trading, who match buyers and sellers. Initially, this was just for **FTSE-100** shares, but is likely to be extended to the **FTSE-250**. **Bid-offer spreads**, rather than being reduced as was thought, actually *increased* especially during trading early in the day.

Blue chip A share in a large, safe, prestigious company. Marks & Spencer is a blue chip, so is the Hong Kong and Shanghai Bank Corporation. Many of the shares making up the FTSE-100 are blue chips.

Bond A bond is essentially a loan. Bondholders lend money to governments or companies and are promised a certain rate of interest in return. Interest rates vary depending on the quality or reliability of the bond issuer. Government bonds, or **gilts**, for example, carry little risk and thus offer lower interest rates. Company bonds offer higher interest rates, with the riskiest companies' (or governments') bonds offering the highest of all and known as junk bonds.

Bonus issue Or, in the US, a 'stock split'. Whenever a company believes that the price per share of its stock has risen to a point where investors may erroneously perceive it as 'expensive', they will split the stock, reducing the price but increasing the number of shares outstanding. For instance, if Huge Fruit Inc. trades at £60 a share with 3 million shares outstanding and decides to split its stock two-for-one, this means that each share will now trade at £30 but there will be 6 million shares outstanding.

Broker One who sells financial products. Be it in insurance, pensions or shares, most brokers work under compensation structures that are at direct odds with the greatest good of their clients. (Also see **execution-only stockbroker**, **advisory stockbroker**, **stockbroker**.)

Bull Are your glasses rose-coloured? Do you see nothing but blue skies ahead for the stock market or a particular security? Then you're a bull – an optimistic investor – as opposed to a **bear**.

Building society A mutual organization, owned by the people saving money in it and borrowing money from it. Increasing numbers have converted to banks in recent years, paying windfall profits to the owners. See **demutualization**.

CAC 40 French **index** of – wait for it – the 40 major French companies.
Capital A business's cash or property, or an investor's pile of cash.
Capital gain You bought a share and later sold it. If you made a profit, that's your capital gain. If you lost money, it's a capital loss. If a member of your investment club is likely to go over their Capital Gains Tax limit through a sale that the investment club is making, then they should contact their local tax office.
Chief executive The chief executive is the highest executive officer in a company, rather like the captain of a ship. He or she is accountable to the company's board of directors and is frequently a member of that board. The chief executive participates in setting strategy with the board and other officers and is responsible for the tactics in meeting the company's goals.
Churn Churning is the unconscious or conscious over-trading by a **stockbroker** in a customer's account. Since stockbrokers are generally compensated by the number of transactions made on a customer's behalf, there is a temptation to trade for the sake of it. It's illegal, but hard to prove.
The City London's financial district, which encompasses the square mile of the old City of London, bounded on the south by the Thames, on the west by the Law Courts, on the east by the Tower of London and in the north by Billingsgate Market.

Commission The way a **stockbroker** or an Independent Financial Adviser is compensated. When he or she makes a transaction for a customer, the customer pays a commission.
Common stock A US term for **shares**.
Compound interest The investor's best friend. One hundred pounds invested in the stock market in 1918 would be worth over £1 million today. Now *that's* compound interest!
Correction: A decline, usually short and steep, in the prevailing price of shares traded in the market or an individual share. Any time that commentators cannot find a reason for an individual stock or the entire market falling, they call it a correction. It sounds better than a 'crash'.
CREST Introduced in 1996, this is a computerized system to settle up share purchases. No more bits of paper passing hands any more.
Cum-dividend: 'Cum' means 'with' in Latin. If you buy shares cum-dividend, you are buying them at a time when you will be entitled to receive the next dividend. This is as opposed to **ex-dividend**. If restrictions on entitlement to dividends didn't exist, people would simply buy shares the day before the dividend was due, collect it and then sell them the day after.
Dax German **index** of major companies, broadly equivalent to the **Dow Jones Industrial Average**.
Day trader: A US term. Day traders are in and out of the market many times during the course of one

trading session and may not even hold a position in any securities overnight. This approach tends to generate a lot of expenses in the form of commissions and denies the day trader the ability to participate in the long-term creation of wealth through compounding which is possible if you own the shares of a quality business.

Demutualization The process **building societies** go through when they convert to banks and thus go from being owned by their members (the borrowers and savers of the society) to being a **Public Limited Company** owned by shareholders. There are pros and cons and the arguments rage on . . .

Derivatives If **shares** are assets, derivatives represent contracts to buy a particular **security** at a given point in the future for a particular price. **Options** and **futures** are derivatives. They can be used to lessen investment risk, but often their main attraction is that they are highly **geared** and can thus offer spectacular profits . . . and spectacular losses. We do not advocate their use.

Discount broker The US term for **execution-only broker.**

Dividend A distribution from a company to a shareholder in the form of cash, shares or other assets. The most common kind of dividend is a distribution of earnings. See **dividend yield.**

Dividend yield The dividend over the current share price, expressed as a percentage. Different companies have different policies on the size of their dividend payouts. See **Beating the Footsie.**

Dow Jones Industrial Average The 30 companies chosen by editors of Dow Jones & Company that are supposed to epitomize the very best American corporations and reflect the landscape of corporate America.

Earnings The money a company puts in the bank after all of the costs of delivering a product or service have been accounted for. See **Earnings Per Share.**

Earnings Per Share (EPS) Net income divided by the current number of shares outstanding. This is one of the principal elements used in determining at what value the shares should trade.

Equities A concept that comes from 'equitable claims'. Equities are essentially shares of stock. Because they represent a proportional share in the business, they are equitable claims on the business itself.

Ex-dividend A share sold without the right to receive the dividend payment which is marked as due to those shareholders who are on the share register at a pre-announced date. These shares have 'xd' next to their price listings in the *Financial Times.*

Execution-only stockbroker Stockbrokers who offer fewer of the services championed by **advisory stockbrokers**, but charge cheaper transaction fees. Basically, you tell them to buy or sell a particular share and they get on and do it with no frills and no hassles. Often they hold your shares in a **nominee account**.

Execution-only brokers are ideal for do-it-yourself investors – that's you. They are called discount brokers in the US.
Exit Charge A sales charge paid for redeeming a unit trust or other investment.
Fair value The theoretical price at which a company is 'fairly valued', meaning that it would not be reasonable to assume that the shares will rise. Fair value at any given point is derived from a number of qualitative and quantitative aspects of the business.
Financial Services Authority (**FSA**) The top investment watchdog. Contact them on 020 7638 1240.
Flotation See **New Issue**.
Fool One who exhibits a high degree of **Foolishness**.
Foolishness The state of being wry, contrary, canny and capable of looking after your own investments. Fools believe in shares as the long-term path to wealth creation and believe in buying and holding good companies for the long haul based on their fundamental financial and business strengths.
FT-30: For many years, the FT-30 was the **index** most often quoted in relation to the London **Stock Exchange**. It was originally conceived as being the UK equivalent of the **Dow Jones Industrial Average**, but is little quoted now. (Except by Fools intent on **Beating the Footsie**.)
FTSE-ASI All Share Index An **index** containing the 900 largest companies on the London **Stock Exchange**. Either the FTSE-ASI, or the **FTSE-100** are

the indices generally tracked by **index trackers.**
FTSE-100 An **index** containing the 100 largest companies by **market capitalization** on the London **Stock Exchange.** Came into being in 1984 and largely superseded the **FT-30.**
FTSE-250: An **index** containing the 250 largest companies by **market capitalization** on the London **Stock Exchange,** created in 1992.
Full-service broker The US name for an **advisory stock broker.**
Futures A type of **derivative** that allows you to bid for the right to pay a future value on either an index option or a commodity. Futures are a great way to lose 100 per cent of your investment, because if they expire worthless you get nothing. Futures have a fixed duration and normally only last for one year at the most.
Gearing Buy a house for £100,000 with a deposit of £10,000 and the rest as a mortgage. Six months later, sell it for £150,000 and you've made 400 per cent profit on your original investment: that's gearing. Of course, it can work the other way too. Gearing can be expressed as the ratio of debt to assets and is used by companies and investing individuals to enhance their profits, as well as homeowners to allow them to buy a home.
Gilts When the government needs to borrow money, it sells you these. They are government **bonds** and as a rule the interest is paid **gross** (i.e. free of tax). They are

very safe and their US equivalent is the Treasury bill, or 'T-Bill'.

Gross The payment of any form of income (interest or dividend payout) without the prior deduction of tax.

Index Groups of shares mathematically reworked to be representative of the current level of the market or of different sub-groups of companies within the market. See **FTSE-100, FTSE-ASI, FTSE-250, FT-30.**

Index Trader An investment fund that invests equal amounts across, say, the **FTSE-100**. This reduces management charges and gives a performance better than 90 per cent of managed funds.

Initial Public Offering (IPO) The US name for a company's first sale of **shares** to the public. In the UK we call it a **new issue**.

Insider dealing This is when you buy or sell a share and at the same time possess privileged information which would move the price if it were widely known. It's illegal, but is also widespread and there are few prosecutions for it.

Institutions Institutional investors include pension funds and unit trusts. These are the big players in the stock market as they have a lot of money to invest and as major shareholders they often have a say in company decisions.

Investment club Group of investors which meets regularly to discuss which shares to buy and sell out of a common fund. See **ProShare**.

Investment trust A Public Limited Company which makes investments into a variety of other companies. Notwithstanding several important differences to **unit trusts**, these are also pooled stock market investment funds.
Large cap See **Market capitalization.**
Leverage The US term for **gearing.**
Listed company A **Public Limited Company** (PLC), listed on a **stock exchange.**
Liquidity The easier it is to turn an asset into cash, the more liquid it is. Shares are very liquid as they can be sold any weekday at any brokerage. Works of art and homes are not nearly as liquid because you need to find an interested buyer. Since every buyer needs a seller and vice versa, **penny shares**, which are very thinly traded, are more *illiquid* than larger capitalization shares.
Margin 1. Borrowing money to use specifically for buying securities of any kind in a brokerage account. 2. A measure of profitability of a company, such as profit margin, operating margin or gross margin.
Market capitalization The total market value of all of a firm's outstanding shares. Market capitalization is calculated by multiplying a firm's share price by the number of shares outstanding. **Large cap, medium cap, small cap** refer to shares in decreasing order of market capitalization.
Medium cap See **Market capitalization.**
NASDAQ National Market A national US stock

market where trades are made exclusively via computers. The second largest market in the country, the NASDAQ is home to many high-tech and newer firms, including Microsoft. It now has its own web site for UK investors: http://www.nasdaq.co.uk

New issue The first time a company is floated on the stock market. Selling your company, or a part of it, to outside investors is a way to raise money for expansion plans.

New York Stock Exchange (NYSE) The largest and oldest stock exchange in the United States, this Wall Street haunt is the one frequently featured on television, with hundreds of traders on the floor staring up at screens and answering phones, ready to trade stocks upon command from their firms.

Nominee account Stockbrokers will often hold shares for their clients as nominees in a nominee account. No certificates are issued to the clients. This is highly desirable for investment clubs, as otherwise shares have to be purchased in the names of individuals and deeds of trust have to be drawn up. There are also problems if the named individuals die, or become unable to manage their own affairs. Nominee accounts solve these problems.

Options Contracts that give a person the right to buy or sell an underlying share or commodity at a set price within a set amount of time. The majority of options expire worthless.

Penny share A share of very low **market capitalization**

(often a few million pounds) trading in multiples of just a few pence. They are very volatile, subject to extreme price fluctuations on the flimsiest of rumours and not at all the thing for the long-distance **Fool**. See **liquidity**.

Price/Earnings ratio (P/E) A measure of a share's price in relation to its trailing twelve months earnings per share. Often, the higher the sustainable growth rate of a company, the higher its price-to-earnings ratio.

ProShare A pressure group representing the interests of the private investor. They publish a magazine called *Dividend*, and also have a useful information pack on how to set up an **investment club**. Contact them on 020 7600 0984, or visit their web site at www.proshare.org.uk

Public Limited Company (PLC) As opposed to private, a company is public after it issues partial ownership of itself, in the form of shares, to the public. Only PLCs can be listed on the London **Stock Exchange** or the **Alternative Investment Market**.

Quarterly reporting In the US, after each quarter-year a company is required to file a report providing investors with juicy details on how the company is doing. In the UK, equivalent reports are seen only every six months.

Revenue The money a company collects from a customer for a product or service. See **earnings**.

Rights issue When a public company creates new

shares. Existing **shareholders** are generally offered the right to purchase a certain number at a discount to the market value. In the US, a rights issue is a form of secondary offering.

Securities Securities is just a blanket way to refer to any kind of financial asset which can be traded.

Security and Exchange Commission (SEC) The United States agency charged with ensuring that the US stock market is a free and open market. All companies with stock registered in the United States must comply with SEC rules and regulations, which include filing quarterly reports on how well the company is doing.

Securities and Futures Authority (SFA) The people who regulate your **stockbroker**. Phone number 020 7378 9000.

Securities and Investments Board (SIB) Now called the **Financial Services Authority**.

Share A **security** which represents part ownership of a company.

Shareholder If you buy even one **share** in a company, you can proudly call yourself a shareholder. As a shareholder you get an invitation to the company's annual meeting, and you have the right to vote on the members of the board of directors and other company matters.

Small cap See **market capitalization**.

Stamp duty A tax you pay on buying shares (0.5 per cent) or buying properties (1 per cent). In the latter case, stamp duty starts to be charged at £60,000.

Standard and Poor's 500 Stock Index (S&P 500) An index of 500 of the biggest and best companies in American industry.

Stock exchange A place where stocks and shares are bought and sold. The London Stock Exchange serves this function in the UK.

Stock split US name for a **bonus issue.**

Stock The same as a **share** and used more commonly in the US. A share of stock (confusing, yes – just use the two interchangeably, everyone else does) represents a proportional ownership stake in a corporation. Investors purchase stock as a way to own a part of a publicly traded business.

Stockbroker A middleman who buys and sells shares on your behalf and earns commission on the transactions. Considered by many to be the fifth-oldest profession after prostitutes, pimps, tax collectors and accountants. See **execution-only stockbroker, advisory stockbroker.**

Symbol An abbreviation for a company's name which is used as shorthand by share quote reporting services and various online sites.

Underwriter/underwritten The **stockbrokers** who help a company come public in a **new issue.** They underwrite (vouch for) the stock. When a company has been brought public, the shares have been underwritten.

Unit Trust A form of managed investment fund.

Most managed investment funds carry high charges and underperform the stock market average.
Valuation The determination of a fair value for a security. If you don't use some reasonable method, then you have what is technically called a 'guess' or a 'hope'.
Wall Street Also known as 'The Street' in US cocktail-party patter, this is the main drag in New York City's financial district.
Yield See **dividend yield.**

INVESTMENT
PROSHARE
CLUBS